The Girl with the Flower
The Journey is the Trip

Janrose Kasmir

First Edition 2020 Fortis Publishing

Copyright © Fortis Publishing under exclusive licence from Janrose Kasmir.

The rights of Janrose Kasmir have been asserted in accordance with the Copyright, Designs and Patents Act 1998.
No part of this book may be reprinted or reproduced or utilised in any form or by any electronic, mechanical, or other means, now known or hereafter invented, including photocopying and recording, or in any information storage or retrieval system, without permission in writing from the publishers.

ISBN-13: 978-1-9163212-9-8

Fortis Publishing
Kemp House
160 City Road
London
EC1V 2NX

This book is a true story. Some names and identifying details have been changed to protect the privacy of the individuals involved.

About the author

Janrose Kasmir is currently living in Hilton Head with her daughter, Lisa Ann Kasmir. She is on the cusp of a new life, wholly dedicated to promoting peace, social justice and higher consciousness.

At seventy, she is leaving a thirty-five-year career as a medically trained massage therapist so that she may pursue her two passions: serving the community and improving her health.

Jan has always aspired to study Judaism with the goal of becoming a rabbi. Her mother received her doctorate in psychology at the age of 52 and considering that Jan comes from a family of late bloomers, it is not beyond the realm of possibility that she may pursue a rabbinical degree.

Time will tell.

For Lisa

Acknowledgements

First and foremost, I want to thank my beautiful, intelligent daughter Lisa Ann Kasmir, who makes me so grateful and proud to be her mother. Truly she is the best of me, and never fails to grace my life with her thoughtfulness.

I must also thank my sainted psychoanalyst, Dr. Herman Arnold Meyersburg. I would never have had a life or a healthy daughter if it were not for his almost 20 years of quality therapy, for which he never took a penny. When I was lost, he salvaged my soul.

To my dear friend and health mentor, Viktoras Kulvinskas. His generous loving care at his sanctuary has kept me alive throughout the years. He kindly nursed me back to health on many occasions with his superior knowledge of nutrition and the healing arts.

Finally, I must thank Ken Scott for all his thoughtful work and guidance. Safe to say, this book would never have existed without his tenacity and guidance.

Prologue

It's a tough business establishing yourself as an author; making a living from writing books is nigh on impossible and the statistics show that less than 3% of all serious authors actually achieve that Holy Grail. But I'm not complaining, as going to work in your boxer shorts with a view of the Mediterranean Sea at an hour of your choosing, surely takes some beating. And there are other far more rewarding experiences than receiving a royalty cheque. Typing 'THE END' on a 200+ page manuscript is one of those moments that warrants the cork being removed from a vintage Rioja or a champagne of your choice. That wonderful occasion when your first book falls into your hands stirs the emotions in even the hardiest of souls. I remember seeing one of my books on a bookshelf in Waterstones in Piccadilly, London and found myself firmly rooted to the spot, unable to do anything other than tremble with pride. I have been fortunate enough to see my books in the *Sunday Times* Top Ten, on one occasion a WH Smith 'Book of the Week' and even saw one of my efforts as the official 'window display,' in one of the biggest book stores in the U.K.

Then there are the reviews and the press articles and sometimes TV and radio requesting opinions and interviews. Although my bank manager may disagree, I've never regretted leaving my real job behind several years ago, as there are never two days the same and always a surprise or two around every corner. I've met (and written books for) people and characters and heroes that the average man or woman could only dream of meeting, and more recently signed a movie option to one of my books.

Some things that happen are simply mind blowing. A couple of years ago a friend of mine sent me an American publication that had featured the '40 most iconic photographs in history'. I sat for some time studying them. They truly were jaw-dropping, many of them I'd seen before and iconic was most certainly the perfect description. Some were poignant like the photograph of a dog that had refused to leave his master's grave, the black power salute at the 1968 Olympics, Jewish prisoners being liberated from the Nazis and John F Kennedy Jr. saluting his father's coffin. Who could ever forget that moving image? Marc Riboud's photograph of the young pacifist and peace demonstrator, Janrose Kasmir, planting a flower in the bayonet of a guard at the Pentagon during a protest against the Vietnam War, was another that strangely stirred something deep inside me. Yet, I didn't have time to dwell on the image because, lo and behold, at number 21 a photograph of Horace Greasley, the WWII prisoner of war, facing up to the biggest mass murderer in history, none other than Heinrich Himmler. My heart fluttered, it possibly missed a beat or two because I had written Horace Greasley's war time memoirs some years ago and the book had become a bestseller. I was speechless. Imagine that, my man Horace as one of the most powerful photographs of all time? Another, but altogether different surprise, and one of those special moments that make this book writing business worthwhile.

The photographs went viral; Facebook and Twitter users posting their own favorites and Horace's book *Do the Birds Still Sing in Hell?* surged into the top ten best-selling books on Amazon yet again. A few weeks passed and occasionally during a hard day's writing and perhaps one or two more glasses of red wine than was healthy, I dreamt the night away. I dreamt of that photo of Horace Greasley and of JFK Jr. and of the little dog at his master's grave, but above all I dreamt of the girl with the flower, Janrose Kasmir; that iconic photo that would become the symbol of the flower power movement. Why did that image come to me more often than any other? I just couldn't explain it.

I'm a firm believer of fate, of things that happen for a reason or quite simply because they are meant to happen. It is said our fate can never be taken away from us, that if you want something bad enough the universe conspires to make it happen. So, although a Skype request from a certain Janrose Kasmir on a wet Wednesday evening bowled me over, I can't exactly say I was that surprised. Janrose had been in my dreams for some time and she messaged me to say she had read one of my ghost-written biographies (*This Heart Within*

Me Burns, Crissy Rock) and that I was the person she wanted to help her with her autobiography. I knew at that precise moment that I would be working with Janrose Kasmir later but there were many bridges to cross. First and foremost, did she have a story and was she as committed as I needed my storytellers to be for anything up to a year? I was also extremely busy with two books in progress as well as a screenplay. Janrose had a few issues at that time too, issues that she talked candidly about, issues that arose from the many tragedies that dogged her life since that iconic picture. Writing a book is a journey I told her, a battle with the demons from the past and a good autobiographer must bare her soul on every page. She admitted that the timing wasn't good, but she did want to tell her story when her own particular planets aligned.

I'm pleased to say that Janrose kept in touch and in March 2015 'our' project began.

Whatever happened to Janrose Kasmir? You're about to find out.

Ken Scott, author and ghost-writer

1

Looking back at my younger years I can't believe the path my life took. Prior to adolescence, everything seemed to be on track for a stereotypical 1950's normalcy. Then tragedy struck, destroying all sense of tranquility, planting the seeds for a new path that was rife with turmoil and tragedy.

Ultimately, that which did not kill me indeed made me stronger, giving rise to a life centered in strength and goodness.

I grew up thinking my family and I were perfectly normal, and I mean normal!

I was born in southeast Washington D.C., in Trenton Terrace, and have no real memories of that place. My first memories are of my family moving to the suburbs of Silver Spring, Maryland, when I was around five years old. It was a beautiful place with woods and a reservoir just beyond our back yard. The backyard lawn stretched to the edge of the woods and featured two or three rows of dogwood trees. Every spring these trees would burst into bloom with large petaled flowers, sporting pink edges and with yellow and green splotches in the center. At some point my father built a small tree house for us at the edge of the woods. Calling it a tree house would grandly overstate it. It was a small triangular wooden platform that was nailed into three trees, about ten feet from the ground. Dad made a ladder by fastening blocks of wood in the tree, so it was easy to access. Altogether the base was about eight feet long on two sides and maybe five or six feet long on the shorter side. It was big enough for a few of us to sit on it with our legs dangling over the sides. With enough imagination, we were able to turn it into a spaceship to fly high in the sky or a pirate schooner to sail around the world. Our imaginations were never limited even a little.

Around the time I was ten, the tree house became the site of my neighborhood's superheroes' fortress. Each of my girlfriends assumed the role of a different comic book superhero. Sandra Katz was Super Girl! Sandra was scrawny and roughly five feet, five inches tall. She created a cape out of a bed sheet she tore up, unbeknownst to her mother. She tied her sheet around her neck and was prepared to fly to wherever danger awaited her. Maureen Mintz, my friend from a few blocks away, was Super Boy. Making a cape from the leftover sheet which Sandra used made the most sense for her costuming. She also sported the sheet tied firmly around her ample shoulders. Maureen was a little more than pudgy, with pin straight black hair that hung to her chin. I was Green Lantern, and though I did not have a costume, I was still special, as I could recite Green Lantern's creed:

In brightest day, in blackest night,
No evil shall escape my sight!
Let those who worship evil's might
Beware my power, Green Lantern's light!

   We would hang out in the tree fort/superhero headquarters and plot the storyline we were going to enact that day. We were the core group, though other neighborhood kids would often take on superhero personas and join in. We spent hours fighting imaginary villains and rescuing the weak and needy. It was a creative and healthy way to spend our energy.
   It is true that sometimes we'd get bored with rescuing imaginary victims, and for those days we had created a more private clubhouse in one of the neighborhood girl's basement. Then, our play would be focused on exposing our vaginas to each other, so we could see how we were alike or different. A few times we would touch each other on a dare. That play abruptly came to a halt when one of the parents suspected something was wrong after noticing her child came home with her pants partially undone. We were banned from congregating alone out of sight after that for a long time.
   I was not immune to other questionable behavior. The first time I tried to smoke cigarettes I was ten years old. I remember walking behind one of the neighbors who was puffing away on a cigarette. She was the mother of one of my school chums and was someone I really liked. I was careful

not to be seen. I was really captivated as I watched her inhale the smoke, hold it and then blow out. It all seemed so easy and fun. It suddenly dawned on me, as I watched her flick the half-smoked butt, that I could get away with trying it if I were quick and sneaky enough. I really wanted to imitate the way she smoked, the way she looked. She went home and I was alone with the butt. I checked out in front and behind me and it didn't seem that anyone was watching me. This was my big chance. I crept over to where the cigarette butt was still glowing. It was as if it called me over and almost begged me to put it in my mouth. I seemed to be in a dream. I picked it up. The filter tip was still wet and had traces of lipstick. Determined to see just what it was that adults enjoyed so much about tobacco, I took a puff. I gagged immediately as the acrid smoke filled my mouth and hit the back of my throat. Gasping for air I threw the butt back into the grass as a sickly bile taste crept up my throat and soured my mouth. The taste of the cigarette induced involuntary spasms in the pit of my stomach and a few seconds later I felt sick. The incredibly vile taste lingered in my mouth throughout the rest of the night and I swore I would never smoke another cigarette again as long as I lived. That vow lasted until I was twelve.

As a pre-teen I wanted to look older and be accepted by my peers, so it was a kind of a rite of passage to smoke. Everyone seemed to. I'd saved up thirty-five cents to buy a pack of Viceroys, the same brand my mother smoked, which I'd hide in my bowling shoes. My mom and dad never looked in my shoe bag because it stank. I'd visit the bowling hall several times a week, puffing away on the forbidden cigarettes.

My mother was five feet, five inches tall, with a round face and short, pin-straight dark brown hair that she wore in a long pixie cut. She always carried an extra twenty pounds, which was a lot for her short stature. She would get pretty fat in her senior years, but never bridged into obesity. My dad was six feet tall, with dark brown thin hair, and a very prominent Jewish nose. It wasn't so big as to be the object of conversation, but I always felt it was a giveaway that we were Jewish. My baby brother Seton grew to six feet when he was in high school. He had thin brown wavy hair that he would worry away into baldness in his adult years. He looked like the product of my parents with his ethnic features, mostly it was the nose. My older sister, Lise, and I looked a great deal alike, though she was only five feet, five inches tall and I grew to five feet, eight-and-a-half inches tall in my late teen years. Lise had the same brown, thin wavy hair all three siblings shared, though Lise and I were spared having a big schnozz. Lise never struggled with her weight the way Seton and I did. She seemed to remain comfortably thin, while Seton had to run to lose weight and I just struggled.

I spent a lot of my early days in those woods at one with nature. My life was quintessentially Jewish and middle-class. I grew up in a middle-class Jewish neighborhood, with Jewish middle-class parents, and Jewish middle-class values. My siblings and I we were four years apart in age, with Lise as the oldest and Seton the youngest. Babette and Charlie were my parents, originally coming to D.C. from Flatbush, N.Y. They left a number of family members back in New York, and I was blessed to go back and visit them at wonderful, culturally rich celebrations: weddings, bar and bat mitzvahs, bris ceremonies (where circumcision is performed by a *mohel* on the eighth day of the male baby's life) and anniversary celebrations that were steeped in Jewish traditions of food, music and Yiddish. All conversations were heavily laced with thick accents from New York or the old country. All the clothing and jewelry were over the top, letting everyone know that these were people with taste, class and above all, money! It was like Neiman Marcus without the hangers.

My mother went to great lengths to ensure that our close friends and neighbors were all Jewish so we could all share the holidays together as a neighborhood. Each family took turns hosting traditional holiday feasts. Passover was the most elaborate as the religious service was intertwined with the enjoyment of food, wine and family.

We always went to Temple on the high holidays, Rosh Hashanah, the Jewish New Year and Yom Kippur, the Day of Atonement. My father had been bar mitzvah-ed, so he fasted every year for Yom Kippur as was the tradition handed down from his parents. However, when it came to my relationship with food, there was no possibility that I could tolerate any sense of deprivation. To me, not snacking between meals was as close to fasting as I could bear.

My dad was a businessman and taught me the value of money and the ethics of hard work and honesty. Unfortunately, he didn't practice what he preached. He was a *gonif*, which is Yiddish for thief. He was completely dishonest with his customers, thinking nothing of ripping them off. He had a small store in Suitland, Maryland, where he sold televisions, air conditioning units and other electrical appliances. He worked six days a week without fail. I remember him never missing a day. The shop was rather dirty, especially in the back workroom, with piles of dust on every surface. The front of the store, that had all the merchandise, was more presentable, but still left a great deal to be desired. The neighborhood was primarily black lower class and pretty rough. Everyone knew my dad, as he had been there for many years, so he was completely safe.

One fond memory centered on a friend of his who owned a pickle shop. Every week or so my father would bring home a huge jar of pickled green tomatoes. I never found another that could come close to those wonderful treats. I can still see the gallon jar brimming with those wonderful tart green tomato slices. I honestly don't remember what they tasted like but given the opportunity I bet I could make a serious dent in a gallon jar.

Another pleasurable memory I have about visiting the shop centers around the merchandise. Anytime I saw something I liked in the shop, I only had to ask my dad, and it came home with me. Radios are the only items I remember getting, though it really wasn't what I got that made the occasion so special. What I vividly recall was the sense of satisfaction and pride I felt that my daddy was the owner and had the power to grant me any wish. I felt like a princess! So special and privileged. I was so proud that he was the big man of the store and I was 'the owner's daughter'. I was somebody.

I actually had the opposite experience when I was in my mother's working world.

My mother was an art teacher. Without fail, whenever I would visit her class, she would make absolutely sure that nobody could accuse her of treating me preferentially. In fact, not only did she avoid any hint of favoritism, she would be sure that whatever the situation, I would be last. Last person called on when hands were raised. Last person to receive materials that were passed out. I was last and least regarded in every instance. She would later explain that she didn't want people to think she played favorites with her daughter. Favorites? It seemed like she hated me. I'm just sorry she wasn't alive to read this book, as I wish I could have talked to her about this. I guess we will just have to confer on the other side when I pass.

Socially, my mother was always the center of attention at any party. She came alive whenever there was a Jewish holiday or other excuse to celebrate. Her favorite occasions were Purim, Passover and Hanukkah. At Purim she usually worked with the Jewish Sunday School to help organize a festival. All kinds of challenging games would be set out, with different degrees of difficulty so that every age would enjoy them. Bean bag toss was always a hit, with the little ones being allowed to practically touch the hoop they had to get the bean bag into. She would help provide costumes she picked up from thrift stores, old prom dresses were a favorite.

At home, Passover topped her list of family favorite celebrations. For Passover we would have large Seders, the Jewish ritualistic meal, complete with a rather extensive reading from the Haggadah, the Jewish book that outlines the stories of our release from the enslavement of Egypt.

One of my favorite games was hiding the *matza*, which is the cracker-like treat that symbolizes the unleavened bread that was accidentally produced by my forefathers in Egypt. When the Jews were told they had to leave their homes immediately in ancient Egypt, there was no time for any bread they were making to rise or leaven. This unleavened bread was baked as is, creating the *matza* we now use to celebrate the holiday.

Traditionally, a piece of *matza* is hidden at the beginning of the Seder, and the young children are invited to find it and redeem it for a financial reward.

My mother's celebrations did not just focus on Jewish holidays, as she loved to throw elaborate parties with her highly creative friend, Anita Werthiem. Anita was a solidly built woman, about five feet, five inches tall, carrying a comfortable bit of fat, very bosomy, with salt and pepper colored hair. For as long as I could remember, creating an event was a way for them to channel their creative energy into a family affair. Anita was a very accomplished artist, mostly painting with oils. My favorite way of describing her creativity was to recall the way she stacked logs in her backyard. She painted faces on the ends of the logs. The top logs had smiley faces. As you went to lower levels, the smiley faces started to show signs of strain. The lower the log, the more strained they looked until you reached the bottom row. They were completely miserable, with bulging eyes looking up at the logs stacked on top of them. This is a tiny example of her highly creative mind, but one that I thought captured her wonderful sense of humor, and the serendipity of her art.

For Anita and my mother, it was as if the celebrations, the times of enjoyment, were there to compensate for the great deal of day-to-day drudgery. Both of them suffered unhappy marriages. Certainly, my teenage years were spent listening to one fight after another. Anita had a good relationship with her son, but I believe there was a great deal of distance between her and her oldest child. She hated her husband and they were divorced after many years of unhappiness.

So, there were always the parties to lighten life up. No matter what the happening was, they could be counted on to produce something a little out of the ordinary. I'll never forget the funny cut-outs they made. I'm sure you've seen the cardboard cut-outs where the character's body is painted wearing a funny costume, but there is a hole where the face should be, and a person can stick his face through to create a comical illusion. The standing cardboard cut-out they made consisted of a 1930's old timer's red and white striped bathing bloomers and a matching cap, under which yellow curls cascaded down over the shoulders. A matching figure representing the male bather was fitted up, so a couple could look ridiculous together. It took a great deal of time and energy but was absolutely worth it. Anything for a laugh.

They had spent several days together down in the basement and wouldn't let anyone in until it was the day of the celebration. We were made to line up blindfolded to wait for the mystery to be revealed. The blindfolds were removed, and I couldn't quite believe my eyes as my mother and Anita revealed the huge cardboard cut-outs they made.

They showed everyone where to place their bodies and their faces and it was quite brilliant and there were cameras at the ready to capture the funny poses. Soon word got around the neighborhood as children and their parents lined up patiently to take their turns behind the structures. My mother and Anita basked in the adulation following a project well done and of course my mother served food and drink to anyone who turned up.

Sadly, Anita would pass away in her early fifties after losing her second battle with breast cancer. She had beaten it once, but then the day came when her doctor informed her that the cancer returned. I spoke with her on the phone just minutes after she finished speaking with her doctor. I remember reacting completely lame as I tried to tell her some jokes, as if getting her to laugh would help. We hung up after a few awkward moments. That was the last time we spoke. I would not see her again in life or death, as I never went to her funeral.

In addition to her passion for entertainment, my mother's art was the love of her life. She studied painting seriously and seemed to sell her work for respectable prices. Her paintings evidenced a great deal of talent, even winning her recognition from time to time when she entered various art shows.

The great benefit of my mother's art classes, for us, was that we always had a vast assortment of art supplies available, and I was able to discover my own talents. Drawing and painting were never my forte. I excelled in handcrafts, particularly fiber art like knitting, crocheting, embroidery, macramé, and so on.

One other bonus in my mother's immersion in the art world was the wide array of art books she owned featuring a healthy assortment of nudes. This satisfied the curiosity of young twelve-year-old minds. I would sneak the naked pictures out of the house and gleefully share them with my friends as we sat giggling while cautiously looking over our shoulders for suspicious adults. My friends all thought it was great fun and I could tell by their overexcited manners that they were truly pushing the boundaries. I kept my cool, it was nothing out of the ordinary for me. My mother held regular art classes in our home and having a nude model was the norm. It was nothing to find a naked body posing for my mother's classes and occasionally I'd pass a naked man or a woman walking down one of our corridors en route to the toilet or into the kitchen for a drink of water. While it is true that they would have a robe on, they often were careless about keeping it closed.

In addition to the painting classes, my mother taught a variety of crafts for the community recreation center. While I loved creating with yarn, working with the other mediums we had were a treat and a challenge. We had a potter's wheel and a copper enameling kiln in the basement. Mom showed me the basics of how to throw a pot and allowed me and my friends to use the wheel any time we wanted. In the far corner stood the copper enameling kiln, and though I never learned any advanced techniques, she would fire my best efforts, creating little pieces of jewelry which I cherished. It was a real blessing to grow up in a house where arts and crafts were such a regular part of my life.

It seemed I always enjoyed making things with my hands and I enrolled in Girl Scouts to learn more. There I learned to knit. Later I taught myself to crochet and macramé, which is textile weaving using knots rather than weaving or knitting. I was told the craft originated from ancient sailors who sold and bartered their works of art once they went ashore. My hands were never idle as I was always sculpting pieces of clay that were plentiful in Mom's magic basement, or I was tucked away somewhere working on projects with yarn. I honestly had a flair for anything that involved my working with my two hands and yet there was something I couldn't do; draw or paint. I tried hard. Given my mother's talents I convinced myself that if I practiced enough, I would get better and her talent would eventually show through me. No such luck.

One day I observed two paraplegic students in my mother's art class. They had hooks for arms. They were sketching beautifully using a large piece of chalk in their toes. That clinched it for me. I quit trying to draw because I was so embarrassed that I couldn't come up to their ability. I stayed away from drawing or painting until I was much older. It wasn't until I was fortysomething when I attempted to draw with my daughter. I was shocked to discover I was fairly good at it.

My family was small, but not by Jewish standards. Seton was the baby. My little brother was four years younger than me and because of the age gap he wasn't much fun to play with. Seton was always a good boy, the silent type, and I'm ashamed to say that I teased him terribly, often to the point where his tears would flow freely. These days we would say that I bullied Seton but, in those days, we never looked at it like that. It was part of growing up, something that could be described as character-building and not much different to the sort of treatment I received from some of the older boys at school. When I was bullied, I would always hit back first and ask for explanations later.

My father never came to Seton's aid. He always said it was something Seton would need to deal with because far worse would come his way in adult life. My dad assured Seton that one day he would be bigger than me and when that happened, he would give me one hell of a beating and I would never bully him again.

It was different with my sister Lise who was four years older. She was great fun to be with and we would always play together, though we did also fight on occasion. I was Queenie and she was Bossy. Those were the names we gave each other when we were playing. We played very creatively, calling on our imaginations to create hours of play. One of our favorite games was 'elevator.' We would pull the doors open from two facing closets in the hall to make a little cubicle. We would use the hose to the canister vacuum cleaner and talk into it and take ourselves to different floors. We'd close the doors and make believe we were getting out on the different floors when the doors opened. 'First floor, ladies' lingerie!'

Usually we were going on a shopping trip to different make-believe department stores. Such a simple, nonsense of a game but one we'd spend hours playing. It would sometimes drive our parents crazy as the closet doors banged and clashed together, often quite late into the evening.

In our bedroom, we'd lay awake together, some nights until very late listening to our parents fight. I never really knew what it was they fought about and although I tried to listen hard, what it was they were arguing about I never figured it out. When we heard their voices, we had this ritual where I would try to get near the door closest to where they were arguing to hear what they were saying and Lise would say, 'Get back into bed'. At first she would whisper it but if I didn't run away from the door and jump back into bed she would keep saying it louder and louder until I became so afraid that my parents would hear her, that I would run back to my room and dive into my bed.

I had a normal childhood with Lise until she hit the teenage years and withdrew from me. I guess we just grew apart and our childhood games didn't appeal to her anymore as she matured.

A big part of why we drifted apart was that she began to enjoy the company of boys. I was absolutely a tomboy and excelled at sports. I was happier climbing trees or playing football than playing with dolls. Of course, there was always one or two boys who gave me a tough time because they thought I didn't belong in their gang which meant that I had to either back down or fight them. And quite honestly, I could beat up almost anybody my age or size. Even if they were bigger than me I never walked away from a scrap. Needless to say, I took one or two beatings but that was extremely rare. Mostly they backed down to my aggression.

I went to a private elementary school that believed in small classes. Sports was featured as an important part of our life lessons. I had no problem competing against guys and in fact was on the first-string baseball and basketball teams and was the only girl who competed in wrestling. I enjoyed and excelled in everything I participated in; sports were a piece of piss and academically I ranked at the top of my class. I would later find out my IQ tested at over 165.

I loved tests and all things competitive. In second grade I entered a science fair and won second prize. My project was on following the development of chicken embryos. The downside of all of this was that I was anything but popular. I was not winning friends. In fact, I was a mostly an outcast. In junior high school, I finally I found a way to feel included into a group. I found music, bands and finally orchestras.

I started my musical training with the soprano recorder, a small wooden flute, in the second grade. In time I played over thirty instruments. By junior high I had studied piano and then went on to study flute and bassoon with first chair National Symphony flutist, Walter Mann, and first chair bassoonist, Kenny Pasmanick. I played in school bands and joined the Montgomery County Youth Orchestra. I even learned glockenspiel, the bells, and joined my high school's marching band.

Even though I felt like I was as normal as the next guy, I sensed that I was somehow very different. From a young age I knew that I moved to the beat of my own drum. Sometime in early elementary school I had an incident with my teacher, Sue, that I read about many years later in a report card. It really spoke to me being in my own world.

Sue was tall and athletic and wore glasses that she chewed on during lectures. She could be supportive, and often expressed a sincere interest in what the kids were doing, but she had a temper.

The report card I found brought back a lot of memories about my attitude towards others back then. On the day in question the lesson in class was a little tedious and I recall Sue standing by the chalkboard rattling on about something that didn't interest me in the slightest. I pulled out my recorder in the middle of class and started playing on it. I was in my own world as the beautiful melody reverberated around the classroom. Sue didn't appreciate my playing, hauled me out in front of the class and whacked me in the head. She really caught me off guard. My report card basically said that I was in my own world with a high disregard for others, which I couldn't argue with.

2

Matthew Groom was the only child of color at the school. What a cute guy. He was on the short side, maybe five feet, five inches tall, with a tight body, built for speed. I cannot recall anything about his color, except that he wasn't light skinned, though I don't believe he was particularly dark. I honestly did not see the color of his skin except to realize he was a 'Negro'. He was the son of the school cook, Mrs. Groom, who was a tiny woman with a huge heart. It wasn't hard to see that Matthew was her son as they bore a striking resemblance to each other. I remember at some point Matthew and I went steady but there was never any kissing or handholding - it was more of a statement of our friendship status. The boy that would prove to be the love of my life at that time was Timothy Green.

Tim had the sweetest face, extremely pale with slightly bucked teeth, and blonde straight hair he wore in a flat top. He was what we would call *zafig*, which is Yiddish for plump, but absolutely athletic with great muscles. I believe we were pitted against each other in a wrestling match, which I lost, but not by much. I was in 5th grade. Tim and I were so crazy about each other that we had a mock wedding officiated by my teacher Sue. (The same teacher who put me on the floor for playing the recorder in class). We got dressed up, Sue said some sweet words, and at the end of the ceremony we broke a glass and yell 'Mazel Tov!' which means congratulations in Hebrew.

I remained quite bored in class, except when I was allowed to pursue my curiosity in science. That seemed to be the only area Sue allowed me free reign. Later, in college, I discovered I had short-term photographic memory, which I mostly used for tests. I only had to look at a page briefly and I could bring it back to mind, reading the answers from memory. Learning came very easy to me and I adored reading. When I found a subject I liked, I would go to my neighborhood library and literally read every available book on the subject, absorbing everything. One of my early interests was mythology. When I finished reading everything I could find on Greek and Roman mythology, I switched to Norse mythology and Indian folklore and such. Reading, and the knowledge that came from it, always fascinated me and I was blessed to retain a great deal of information. Early on, I began to take notice of the world around me, in particular the issues of the time and the injustices that appeared to be taking place in America. I could see something was terribly wrong about segregation. As I entered my teenage years I became more enlightened about the issues and the players, particularly Dr. Martin Luther King. He became a hero of mine.

I sincerely felt bad about how black people were treated. In elementary school, for Show and Tell, I brought in an article which detailed how young black teenagers, many of them college students, were participating in a lunch counter boycott in Greensboro, North Carolina. I suggested that we should participate, even though I had no idea where Greensboro or even North Carolina were.

Matthew seemed very interested in what I had to say. It was strange because there were no racial problems in our school. If anything, we were colorblind. Everyone got along with Matthew and everyone loved his mama. Both were cherished and admired for their talents. Matthew was an incredible athlete, and everyone loved his mama's cooking and kindness. I felt a little uncomfortable when I spoke about the article on segregation with Matthew sitting in the class, listening to it, staring at me. Deep inside, I was proud that I was bringing up the issue of racism in our classroom.

Although Lise sometimes looked at me as a nuisance (particularly when boys were around), she was beginning to change. I became less important as she took up the cause.

About the time she was fifteen a monumental episode in her life would shape the rest of her life and to this day I still refer to her as the white Rosa Parks.

Rosa Parks was an African American rights activist and the mother of 'The Freedom Movement'. It was in 1955, in Alabama, when Rosa refused to give up her seat on a segregated bus to a white passenger and was arrested for civil disobedience. As a result, she became an international icon of resistance to racial segregation and the incident would prove to be a springboard to her ongoing campaigning against the Jim Crow race laws of the time.

Lise was on a Greyhound bus to visit our relatives in Dallas, Texas when the she was confronted by the ugly issue of racism. Her response to the situation brings me a great sense of pride and admiration. Lise was minding her own business, reading a book as the bus passed the Mason-Dixon line. She happened to notice an elderly black woman who had boarded the bus, looking for somewhere to sit. She wasn't the best at walking and as the bus started up with a lurch, she quickly settled on a seat next to a young white soldier in uniform. The soldier stared at her with a look of disgust and shouted up to the bus driver in the front that he didn't want 'that woman' sitting next to him. Lise was horrified and stood up without a moment's hesitation.

'There's a seat here next to me,' she said loudly. 'I'll be only too happy for the lady to sit here.'

The poor old woman smiled, struggled to her feet with an oversized shopping bag and waddled up the bus towards Lise, where she sat down, grateful to take the weight off her feet. Lise would later say that they just made small talk on the trip but something inside her had been changed forever. She couldn't believe the soldier's attitude towards the poor old lady who was probably old enough to be his grandmother. All of this hate, because she wasn't white. It made no sense.

It wasn't long before the bus stopped at a rest area where my sister's eyes opened to the ugliness of segregation. In the toilet area the washroom facilities were segregated into 'Whites Only' and 'Colored Only.' My sister was horrified. She couldn't believe it and made a stand there, insisting on only using the colored facilities. How I wished I had been there that day to bear witness to Lise's bravery. One can only imagine how filthy and disgusting the 'Colored Only' facilities were, but it mattered not. Lise was prepared to make a stand at any cost. I can just imagine her stubborn but proud face as she stood side by side with the colored women who must have wondered what on earth was going on. And as she walked past the mutterings and stares on the bus, her head held high, she was already planning her next move.

When Lise returned home she started a civil rights group with Jewish friends in the neighborhood, together with some young black friends. I remember some good-looking black teenage boys that were involved and it seemed to me that some of them were more interested in drinking the wine Lise snuck past my parents than they were in plotting to save the world. Since I was nothing more than a nuisance, I was completely banned from every meeting and wasn't allowed anywhere near them.

I tried to sneak a peek into the room at every opportunity and tried to eavesdrop on what was being said but had no luck. One night, however, when it was stiflingly hot, they left the door ajar and I could see in without them noticing. If I suspected something boring, I was wrong. The first part of the evening was spent making candle holders from Chianti bottles: they would drip multi-colored wax candles down the sides of the bottles, then stick a big candle in. Once they started drinking wine, things heated up. Mostly it was white Jewish teenage girls sitting on the laps of these good-looking black teenage boys, making out and sexually teasing them. Of course, they were supposed to be discussing politics, but I guess that was saved for another day. I'm sure they intended to pay attention to the race issues of the time, but it seemed that discussing plans of action around protesting would have to wait. For now, I believe they were drinking, enjoying each other's company and feeling good about making the world a better place, one sexy young man at a time! Although I don't think a whole lot of political action happened as a result of their meetings, I couldn't help but admire my sister and couldn't wait to grow up so that I could be involved in her group. I believed in her core purpose and couldn't wait for my turn.

Lise was getting curious about life outside of our area. In many respects our town and her environment were boring to her. She heard about the beatniks in New York, and outrageous scenes in Greenwich Village. She wanted to go there on her own and check it out. One evening she announced she wanted to go to New York, traveling on her own. I don't honestly remember why she wanted to go, but at just fifteen years of age there was no way my parents would allow it. The fight took place upstairs in our room. It was just her and my dad, both screaming at the top of their lungs. I was downstairs in the den, trying to ignore it all. My father left our room, slammed the door and stormed downstairs. Within a few minutes, my sister started screaming for my father. Her tone went from anger to fear as she pleaded with him to help her.

We lived in a split level. I had moved from the den to the living room couch on the same floor.

Hearing Lise's cry for help, my father raced back upstairs, to find her sprawled on the floor, lying on her back, gasping for air. I ran upstairs to join them. I looked at my father and we both knew instantly something was terribly wrong. My father instantly began CPR on Lise, directing me to hold her writhing legs. I did the best I could.

My mother was close behind us and as she ran into the room and saw poor Lise she became hysterical, and began shouting and screaming. My father turned around to Mom and shouted, 'Get an ambulance here as quick as you can!'

I stayed with my father and could hear my mother downstairs.

She ran to the kitchen phone and I remember her having quite a bit of difficulty trying to find an ambulance. This was before the days of 911, so there was a lot of confusion. Mom was panicking and the simplest of questions seemed to take her an eternity to answer. Finally, she hung up and after what seemed like forever the ambulance arrived. It was the most awful sight in the world, watching the ambulance pull up to our house, something that seemed completely alien, something I had seen happen to other families but never mine. I realized that something truly awful was unfolding and the sight of the ambulance made me realize just how serious the situation was. The ambulance attendants collected a few large cases from the back of their vehicle and rushed into the house. I heard one of them mention a resuscitator and wondered what that meant. It became clear to me what a resuscitator was as they moved my dad out of the way and placed a mask on Lise's face. I couldn't stay in the room. The sounds and sights were too much for me and I ran downstairs to the outside in a frenzy. People had started to gather on our front lawn, curious about why an ambulance came to our house. I didn't know what to do with myself. I could hear the resuscitator's sound coming from the open bedroom door. It was loud and ugly and seemed to exaggerate the sound of Lise's breathing. It was as if the noise took over the house, I could hear nothing but that resuscitator. I was panicking. More people gathered on the lawn and I couldn't stand their prying curiosity. I was furious with their morbid intrusion in my tragedy. I screamed at the top of my lungs. 'This isn't a circus! There's nothing to see, so get out of here!'

Some did, but most remained. They just look like a blur. I could not focus on any individual. They fused into an ugly mob. I stood for some time, then walked back into the house. I managed about twenty minutes and then the sound of the resuscitator again became too much for me. This time I ran out the back door into the woods. I just needed to escape the sound of my sister's breath. Our next-door neighbor, Rachel, ran after me and when she caught up with me, she offered warmth and consolation. Putting her arm around me, she walked me back to her house. Rachel was a tiny woman, barely five feet tall, with a petite frame, and had a head of dark brown curls which I now buried my face in. She wrapped both arms around me. Even though she was small she was my tower of strength at that time. I felt comforted by her strong presence. I kept asking her if Lise was going to be okay. She assured me everything would be fine.

It didn't take long before they took Lise away in the ambulance. I wasn't sure if that was a good sign or not. It was all too much for me. They took Lise to Holy Cross Hospital in Silver Spring Maryland, and she was put in the intensive care unit. She stayed in there for a night and two days. I honestly don't remember what I did at that time. I was not allowed to visit her, and I had no idea of what was happening.

I remember nothing, save one very important event. I believe this event was critical in forming a great deal of guilt which would lead to self-destructive behavior later in my life.

I was sitting in the bathroom upstairs. I watched as a fly landed on the bathtub. I said in my mind, 'G!d, whatever you do to that fly, I want you to do to Lise.'

I had no further thought, but I mindlessly picked up a newspaper that was laying nearby, rolled it up and killed the fly. Without thinking or hesitation.

I buried this memory for many decades.

It took many years of psychoanalysis before the memory was uncovered and I could confront the feelings of guilt that came with the myth of blaming myself for 'killing' my sister. With the help of my brilliant psychoanalyst, Dr. Herman Meyersburg, I understood how I transformed a myth into a powerful sense of guilt I needed to punish. Powerful stuff.

My aunt Audrey flew in from New York to be with us and comfort my mother.

Aunt Audrey had always been my idol. She was tall, five feet, seven inches, with a small waist and ample bust. I always compared her to Veronica from the Archie comic books. Veronica and Audrey have both been blessed with incredible measurements. Audrey had thick, luxurious auburn hair that cascaded past her shoulders. She married a successful lawyer who gave her everything possible materially. They had a huge Tudor house in New Rochelle, New York's suburbs, a summer house in the beach resort of Fire Island, New York, and every comfort I could imagine. Audrey always dressed in the best of fashion. I thought she lived a dream come true. Later she would get divorced, so I can only wonder if her husband was unable to give her more than material things. I was always happy to see Audrey, even if the occasion was dire.

On the third night of Lise's stay in hospital, my parents returned home late. They had been with Lise all day. They were sullen, and my mom and Aunt Audrey seemed to be crying a great deal. I wanted Lise to come home and did not understand why she couldn't. After a couple of hours watching my family sit in silence, I went upstairs to my empty room. I lay awake in bed for hours listening to the adult conversations that started after I left, drifting up through the floorboards. At first, I tried to concentrate hard on what they were saying but in the end I gave up and closed my eyes. It was no good, I couldn't sleep. In the early hours of the morning a phone call came. I instinctively knew it was bad news...

By the time I made it downstairs everybody was up. Dad was on the phone and Mom and Aunt Audrey went over to the couch, sitting and holding each other. The phone call was from Dr. Stiller, our family pediatrician. My father's face was ashen. He thanked the doctor several times, said he understood and that he would call him first thing. He placed the receiver on the hook and turned to face us. I was sitting on the large couch next to Mom. Everyone knew what that phone call meant, but not a word was said. I remember trying to make lame jokes to make everybody laugh, it was as if I was trying to hold off the reality of what was happening. If I could make them laugh, then surely the painful truth could not be realized. After chattering away for a few minutes, I just stopped. I was shaking uncontrollably.

Dad spoke. 'There were complications,' he said. 'Lise just slipped away.'

Slipped away? I'll never forget those words; they were so final.

My mother and Audrey looked at each other, and Auntie Audrey just said, 'Oh, Babs.'

I confess that I can't recall anything after that, nothing at all about the rest of the morning or the entire day. Lise had died of a cerebral hemorrhage which in turn had closed down her breathing center.

For many days my head was filled with visions of the fights I used to have with Lise, all the horrible things I'd said to her and the names I'd called her. Occasionally the fights had turned from harmless words to real violent confrontations, fist fights and slapping and hair pulling, and I'm sad to say that I won most of them, despite the age difference. I felt every punch, every kick and I recalled the time my parents said I nearly killed her. Unbeknownst to me, Lise had an enlarged spleen and during one particularly nasty fight I hit her just below the rib cage. It was a hard blow that caused her to bend over and cry out in pain. Having heard the noise, my parents stormed into the room. They started yelling at me, saying I could have killed her. 'Her spleen,' Mom said. 'is swollen. She has mononucleosis.'

I swear I did not even know what a spleen was or what it did. And what the hell was mononucleosis? I could have killed her? What was that all about? I dismissed it at the time. Later those accusations were taken to heart and tormented me for years.

Our house overflowed with flowers and fruit baskets. I didn't know so many people cared enough about us to send flowers and fruit. These gifts became a source of guilty pleasure. I loved the gifts, but they brought pain as much as any other feeling. I didn't really understand what was going on.

I asked my father if I could just pretend that Lise went to New York, rather than face the fact that she was dead. It was April 22 when Lise died and the cherry blossoms in Washington D.C. were in full bloom. She passed one day after sixteenth birthday. She would be painfully missed.

3

I went on a complete downward spiral after Lise's death. I had a great deal of guilt, blaming myself and our many fights for making her unhappy. My horror would come back to me night after night in the most painful nightmares imaginable. I wasn't the only one to be affected. My parents went through the agony that can only be understood by parents who have lost a child. Lise had so much to give to the world, it shouldn't have happened.

It feels so terribly wrong for parents to bury their children.

Dr. Stiller also took my sister's death very badly, and although there was nothing he could have done to prevent her death, he suffered the loss with us. The Stiller family were close friends of ours, often coming out with us on our boat, and sharing other social occasions. I remember my parents telling me that Dr. Stiller stopped charging for any services after Lise died.

My life was terribly unhappy after Lise passed. I suffered severe depression. I remember sleeping a great deal for no apparent reason and eventually my parents were so worried they took me to see Dr. Stiller, who prescribed a tranquilizer. When I wasn't sleeping, I was very shaky, trembling all the time and, quite frankly, my memory of the period after Lise's death was a complete blur. I think taking those pills interfered with my memory significantly.

Another important factor was that I had just entered puberty. That has its own host of problems with role changes and physiological changes, like hormones. Adding to the natural trauma of that transitional time and the impact of Lise's death was the inept way in which my family handled everything. While I know my parents did the best they could, it still set me up for tough times.

I had no energy at all, lost all interest in sports that I had previously loved and as a result gained weight, not tremendous but enough to make me feel fat. On top of all the emotions frying my brain I now had to contend with hating my appearance and losing all confidence. I was taller than the other kids which made me stand out from the crowd but now I was convinced I was fat too. I was extremely self-conscious about my body, so much so I felt almost freaky, as if everyone hated my looks and me with them.

I went back to Dr. Stiller for more help. He ended up giving me diet pills, Dexedrine. The combination of tranquilizers and diet pills at fifteen was not understood to be inappropriate. I held off on the Dexedrine and tucked the prescription away in my wallet. I didn't want to take it, but I held onto the script in case I changed my mind.

The stimulation I was looking for came in a place called Dupont Circle. I'd heard about it from a group of friends who persuaded me to tag along, as it was 'the coolest place to hang out'. It was in northwest Washington D.C. It started life as a traffic circle, Washington's answer to New York's Washington Square.

The first time I went to check it out, a guitar player and a banjo picker were hanging out on the circle's grass. As I walked towards the center of the circle, I saw a large elegant fountain. There were places for people to sit everywhere. Tables had been set up with chessboards painted on their tops and plain benches were everywhere for people to sit on. And that is exactly what we did. It was the world of the hippie and even though I didn't know what a hippie was, I soon found out because the hippies dominated Dupont Circle. It was the 1960's and they came to read their poetry and spread the love.

I was absolutely fascinated and watched with admiration as these exotic, good-looking young men with beards and loose-fitting blue bell-bottom jeans, jean jackets and other natural clothing stood and captivated their audience with poetry. Their words were meant to inspire others to rebel against the injustices of the system. They would spontaneously stand up and recite their heart songs. They all hated war and agreed that Love was the answer.

There were not too many performance artists in Washington back in those days, but when they recited their poetry and spoke loudly and long enough, it wouldn't take long for a group of people to hang around them and listen. Some of those poems blew me away. I could sit and listen for hours and was in awe of how sensitive and caring these people were. Their badge of courage was their long hair. That identified them as 'one of us'.

The girls wore little or no make-up at all, their jewelry was mostly derived from Native American silver and turquoise. Almost everyone was barefoot and natural and sported long hair, boys and girls alike. They didn't seem to have a care in the world (apart from their causes) and I so wanted to be like them in every way.

They went beyond the beatniks' philosophy and were way cooler. It seemed the beatniks revered poetry and socialism. The hippies were avowed non-conformists that swore off materialism. The root of all evil was greed, primarily corporate greed. Being a piggy was the basest form of existence. The hippies believed in Love as the root of all goodness. We were all brothers and sisters in this universe and were here to share resources and support each other. They got many of their ideas and ideals from mystical thought. Their heroes were people like Mahatma Gandhi, Dr. Martin Luther King Jr, Caesar Chavez, Eldridge Cleaver and Woody Guthrie; socialists who fought for the working person and more. They turned their backs on materialism and vowed to share their worldly goods with others. To that end they formed crash pads and communes where anyone that needed a place to stay could spend a night.

The more I went to Dupont Circle the more I felt as if I belonged. One Saturday I took a D.C. transit, got off near 22nd and P, N.W. and walked over to see if there was anything happening. There was a tall skinny guy who was sharing his melodious poetry. I was completely hooked. He went on about clouds and birds and of course what it was like to fall in love. The poetry was beautiful, I remember thinking what a waste it was to be reciting this to a few individuals, and that he was quite simply the greatest poet on the planet. As he spoke, I couldn't help thinking that he focused on me perhaps more than any other standing around him. I shook it off; I was surely mistaken. But no, I had been right because when he closed his notebook and took a small round of applause, he walked straight over to me and asked me my name. I couldn't believe this guy was talking to me. I was so thrilled.

We talked for ages, sitting on one of the wooden benches until my backside was numb. Finally, he stood up. 'I'll show you my room,' he said, and motioned for me to follow him.

I didn't even think he was inviting me over for sex, though I would have been thrilled at the thought that he desired me. I couldn't get to my feet quick enough. I was so happy walking over to his small rented room. It was nothing special but to me it was heaven because he had invited me there and he was treating me like I was special. I still felt too tall and fat but each minute I spent with him those feelings seemed to evaporate. His name was Les, or at least that is what I remember. The flat was sparse, just a futon on the floor and colored bedspreads in front of the windows, with a record player on a chair. A typical hippie flat. We talked and talked and somehow the conversation got around to the Dexedrine in my wallet. I have no idea how that came into the conversation, but he was instantly riveted on it. When I mentioned that I had the prescription, his face lit up.

'Come on,' he said, without missing a beat, 'find the script and we are going to the pharmacy.'

'I don't understand,' I said as I rummaged through my wallet, looking for the paper my doctor gave me. I found the script and waved it.

'We can get the pills from the pharmacy on the corner.'

I was confused. Les was so skinny I could not imagine what he would want with a prescription for something that helped you lose weight. Then he explained that Dexedrine was great fun; it would give us a real buzz he said. This was my introduction to drugs as a form of recreation. Later I would realize that drugs could re-create me, in that they could significantly alter my psyche so that I seemed to become another person.

I remember it was just a short walk from his place to the drugstore. I walked up to the pharmacist and presented my prescription. It took only a few minutes for the pharmacist to hand me a bottle full of pills, and we were off, back to his pad. Les was so impatient, I practically had to run to keep up with him. Back at his place we opened the bottle and I took two tablets. I remember him looking at me and shaking his head as he laughed. I handed him the bottle and told him to take whatever he wanted. He shook out a bunch into his hand, swallowed all, put the cap back on the bottle and handed it back to me. I stuck it in my purse as I lay back on the floor and relaxed. Les was chilling, just waiting for the effects to kick in.

Mostly, I remember him talking non-stop, but not much else. Nothing remotely sexual happened, which was fine, because I was still a virgin.

Before the pills kicked in I listened to his poetry, but within thirty minutes of ingesting those pills I discovered why he could not control his need to talk and talk and talk and talk because now I was doing the same. G!d knows what was going on in our heads as we talked. He recited more poetry. I could barely listen, as I wanted to talk as well.

After what seemed like an eternity, I left. It was dark out and I needed to get home. I had been in his apartment for hours and was still on a high when I got home. I couldn't wait to tell my mother about all these amazing feelings I had going through my body and my mind. I was totally ready to be a new and better person. I called myself Jan Two, to distinguish myself from my old bad, fat and misbehaving self. I had developed a new confidence within hours, and I truly loved myself for it.

When I got home, I could not stop talking. Looking back, I realize it was the amphetamine affecting me, but at the time I did not understand that. I was in a drug-induced euphoria and that was all that mattered to me. I knew I had been an angry, unhappy child and felt very out of control but at that precise moment there seemed to be a window of opportunity. I felt a glimmer of hope that I could change into a better person and spent all night talking to my mother trying to convince her of that. Finally, in the wee hours of the morning my mother could not stay awake any longer, and later she just crashed. I sensed she was happy that I was making all these promises to reform myself into a better person.

There was so much confusion around the Dexedrine. We both knew my doctor had given me the pills, so we supposed we could trust what was happening. Both my mother and I suspected the crazy part was not good, like when I couldn't stop talking. What I didn't share with her was how I hallucinated tiny flower-laced bras that floated before my eyes, right next to the tiny floating seahorses. Not normal.

She brought a cot into my bedroom and lay next to me. I remember her falling asleep with a smile on her face. That didn't stop me talking; it was impossible to keep quiet. I ended up talking to myself out loud. After a while of watching the hallucinated parade passing before my eyes, I realized why Les wanted those pills so badly. This was fantastic, but at some point exhaustion took over and I finally fell asleep.

That morning the effect of the pills had mostly worn off and I felt groggy and depressed. I later learned that the crash was the price you paid for the fun. I knew at that point that it wasn't that I had changed inside, I realized it had been the pills all along. It was my first drug-induced experience and I recognized that there were problems. The pills made me feel happy and optimistic, so it seemed a fair tradeoff. I wanted that feeling back, I wanted more Dexedrine and I wanted it quickly, and I wanted to share my experiences with Les. It was all so easy, after all I had a perfectly legal prescription from my doctor.

Later that day the effect of drugs wore off completely and I went back to my miserable depressed self, Jan One. I knew I wanted to have that good feeling back. I was starting that slide into addiction. This would be the beginning of a torturous relationship with drugs.

4

The introduction to drugs had a profound effect on my entire being and I found myself changing in the way I thought. I seemed to analyze everything I did. I seemed to try and understand but found myself unable to change my behavior or be happier. Except when I was high. I was able to make small, temporary changes at times. I ate a little less or cleaned my room a little more. I was unhappy with almost every aspect of my life, including the way I looked, and the drugs seemed to temporarily take that away from me. And yet I knew I couldn't pop pills forever. I knew it was not the answer to everything.

From an early age I had a passion for doing good and I recognized that it made me feel good much the same way getting high made me happy. It wasn't that I consciously understood that I needed to do good things to feel good. I just grabbed the opportunity to do something good when it came my way. I would never say no to an invitation to help. Even at that early age I knew that drugs were not the answer and that my only chance out of the downward spiral was to concentrate more on the natural, everyday things that made me feel good. I didn't know that the brain produced certain chemicals that could turn my pursuits and struggles of life into pleasure. I just intuitively gravitated towards volunteering myself to help others.

So, at the age of fifteen I started volunteering for the Red Cross Candy Striper program. The hospital volunteers were called Candy Stripers because of the red and white striped uniforms they wore. My first tour of duty was in a nursing home in Wheaton, Maryland. No one could have prepared me for what I saw. From the moment I walked through the door I witnessed gross neglect of the elderly. Maybe that standard of care was acceptable at the time, but it was pretty horrible, and it pained me to see people treated like that. The poor residents looked like lost souls. There were even wards where some of the people were tied to chairs all day, only being removed when the stench from their waste they were sitting in got someone's attention. I remember walking into one such ward and had the urge to walk straight back out again. I turned to the lady who was showing me around and pointed to one of the old ladies tied to her chair,

'How long will she be tied up like that?' I asked.

She shrugged her shoulders. 'All day.'

And by way of an explanation she said that it was for her own safety.

I took a deep breath. It was the post I was offered, and these poor people needed my help, so I took it. I really wanted to help, surely these people deserved a better life than this and so I started.

On the surface the staff appeared nice enough but in fact the workers looked right through the residents as if they weren't there. Staffers would hold conversations between each other, sometimes standing just a few feet away from a patient, and talk about very personal things, acting as if the resident didn't exist. It would amaze me to the point where I just had to say something, but it never made any difference. So, I concentrated on trying to stimulate the residents by having normal adult conversations with them.

I remember one day clearly, it was fairly early on in my time volunteering there. It was a normal day and I was helping by interacting with the residents. I would try to make small talk or get them some juice. It wasn't that difficult to bring a smile to their faces or to cheer up one of the small groups they sat in. I suddenly noticed that there was a commotion between some of the staff and one elderly resident. She was quite tall and large, with grey hair pulled back in a bun, though her hair was now a bit disheveled. She was terribly upset, talking loudly and gesturing to the staff. Judging by her body language she was growing more and more frustrated and very angry. As I listened, I realized that I could not understand a single word she was saying. One of the staffers explained to me that she was Italian and spoke no English and none of the staff spoke Italian. I immediately sympathized with the poor old woman and understood how upset and alone she must have felt. With each passing moment she became more and more upset.

'Surely somebody can speak a few words of Italian?' I asked. My question fell on deaf ears.

I wracked my brain to think of a few words in Italian, but it dawned on me that the only Italian I knew were food words. It was so frustrating but surely, I could at least try that. I sensed that the old lady's frustration stemmed from the fact that she couldn't get anyone to understand anything she said. Perhaps if she heard a few familiar words it might just calm her down.

So, I walked over to where she was. 'Lasagna.' I said.

She stopped and turned towards me. 'Lasagna!' she said with a big smile.

The staffers looked at me as though I was from another planet, but my little old lady was smiling and that was all that mattered to me.

'How do you make lasagna?' I came back, motioning with my hands a mixing bowl kind of action. Although she didn't understand the first part of the sentence, I think she worked it out. Her response was completely unintelligible to me, but whatever she was saying, it seemed to calm her down as I nodded and said, 'Si, si.'

Though I could not understand the bulk of what she was saying, it was peppered with lasagna, as she no doubt was explaining to me her grandmother's secret recipe on how to make the best lasagna outside Rome. If only. When her conversation started to slow down, I realized I would need to speak in Italian once again in order for the conversation to continue.

'Minestrone!' I said.

Once again, the relief swept across her face, as she went on and on, ostensibly about minestrone and no doubt another fabulous recipe. At this point I sat down with her and took her hands in mine. I listened to her, smiled a lot and nodded, indicating that I understood her and when she would seem to run out of things to say, I would chime in with another Italian dish, like pizza or cannelloni, and off she went again. I could not understand why at least one or two of the staffers hadn't bothered to pick up an Italian phrasebook and learn a few words of Italian. It was clear that what this lady needed was a sense of connection. My conversation with her in her native language, as little as it was, provided a connection. By the time I left she was calm and doing well. One of the staffers said it was the best they had ever seen her. That night when I got home, I looked into my mother's eyes and promised her that I would never allow her to go into a nursing home.

During the six months I volunteered at the nursing home I felt good about myself but for the rest of my waking hours I was still horribly depressed. I felt fat and unattractive, big and unwanted.

There was a thirty-five-year old Spanish guy who worked at the nursing home who started paying attention to me. He would follow me around and ask me to take long walks through the grounds of the home and after a few of these walks he started to hold my hand. When he was sure that we were out of sight of the home he would turn around to face me and kiss me, gently at first but then more and more passionately. It felt good even though I knew he was much too old for me. He never pushed it any further than kissing because I guess he figured out that since I was just fifteen, he would get in big trouble if he we were caught.

Eventually, I don't know how, his wife got suspicious. I remember a big fat woman showed up at work. She was about his age, possibly a little older and I heard my name mentioned as she talked to one of the staff. She turned and looked over, started staring me down and I put two and two together. Although it was all rather harmless, I also realized that it wasn't something a wife would want to find out about and from that day on he never bothered me again. I knew he was too old for me, but I was just relieved that some male wanted me and saw me as attractive. I actually missed our secret rendezvous and once again experienced the pain of loneliness and depression. Despite my good work in the care home I went on a real downward spiral and thought more and more about Lise. I thought about suicide and wondered what it would be like on the other side, the place where Lise was. Surely it couldn't be worse than this?

Day after day I woke up praying that this would be the day that things would change but it never did. Each day was as depressing as the day before and eventually I wanted to do something to end the pain. The only way I knew to end the pain was to end my life. Death didn't seem real to me; it was just a place where Lise was. I thought I wanted to kill myself, but what I really wanted to do was kill the pain. I decided to take some sleeping pills that belonged to my mother. I had seen them in her medicine cabinet. They were yellow jackets, Nembutal. Finally, I took them from the cabinet. I walked casually back to my bedroom, unscrewed the top of the bottle and one by one popped them into my mouth and swallowed. Five, six, seven, eight. Although I was swallowing the pills whole, they still left a bad taste in my mouth and after no more than thirty seconds I became scared. I wanted to stop taking them but the urge to die was greater. I couldn't stop, I wouldn't stop, I wanted the pain to go away and surely this was the easiest way? I took almost the entire bottle, but for some reason held on to two of them. I decided that if I were found, I would show the pills so that it could be determined exactly what I had taken. As I looked at the empty bottle on the carpet, the idea of being dead was suddenly terrifying. Lise's death came flooding back, the flashbacks of the pain and torment both for my parents and me. I was feeling drowsy now and I definitely didn't want to die. My mother was downstairs. I needed to get to her. I stood up. The room was spinning, and I so wanted to collapse onto the bed and sleep forever. I made it to the door and opened it. Everything appeared to be happening in slow motion and I wondered if I would make it downstairs. What if my mother had gone out into the back yard, or to a neighbor's house for coffee? They would find me dead and it would be too late and now I was petrified and knew I had to fight for survival. I almost floated down the stairs and found my mother in the kitchen. She stood by the sink; her figure was a blurred silhouette against the bright sunshine that shone through the window. I said nothing, showed her the two pills and the empty bottle and then I collapsed on the floor.

When I came to, I was in the intensive care unit at Holy Cross Hospital, the same hospital my sister had died in. It was about 3am, I could see the beltway from my window. There were a few cars driving in the early morning drizzle on the beltway, headlights stretched out in front of them, silhouetted by the rain. I was pretty dizzy, and despite trying to fight it quickly fell back to sleep.

When I awoke again, I felt dopey, almost to the point of being drunk. My parents were there by my bedside, somber but not at all angry like I expected them to be. The first thing I thought of again was that this was the very hospital where Lise had died and although I half expected a lecture, it never came. We left as soon as I dressed. We had shared perhaps a dozen words until I arrived at home, and I disappeared into my bedroom, still groggy. I just wanted to be left alone to sleep.

This episode prompted my mother to enroll me into group therapy at the Community Psychiatric Clinic in Bethesda Md, supervised by Dr. Vata.

Dr. Vata was a short, pudgy middle-aged guy with black glasses and thinning hair. He was very quiet. He would occasionally puff on a pipe during group meetings. Rarely would he say anything, even if a group member was in the throes of a self-destructive tantrum. He seemed to think it was our responsibility to make sure the other group members did not hurt themselves.

I felt I had no option but to attend the clinic as I was wracked with guilt at what I had done to my parents. Losing one child was bad enough, and to put them through it all again was something I couldn't live with, so I obeyed my mother and did not object to attending group therapy. She said it would be good for me; a weekly group where we would talk about our feelings with Dr. Vata and the rest of the group. It seemed like a good idea. I wanted to tell other people what I was feeling deep down inside, and I wanted to hear from the other group members if they were experiencing the same pain I did.

I did want to take a moment to talk about one of my favorite group members, Peter Dick.

Yes, that was his real name! He was so hot. He was lanky, with jet black hair he always wore slicked back, like a greaser.

He had the bluest eyes in die world, piercing and beyond sexy. I knew him before we got to the group. He was always cool with me, treating me like a true friend. I always felt he had my back.

My favorite story about him, he told me happened when he was about fifteen. He got caught by a couple of cops in a parking lot, drinking. The one cop really seemed to have it in for him, though he had never seen either one before that night.

'What's your name, son?'

Peter tried very hard to keep a straight face, but he replied with an obvious smirk on his face. 'Peter Dick.'

'Real funny. Now cut the shit or this will get serious. What's your name?'

'Peter Dick.'

'You've got one more chance to cut the shit or I'm taking you into the station.'

Poor Peter. He extended his hands, wrists together, and said, 'Just take me.'

He honestly never felt his name did anything but get him in more trouble.

So, back to the mess the group was. We really did not have any expectations that the group was going to make our lives better. We went because our parents made us. The experience was an utter catastrophe. The group was completely out of control. It was noisy and undisciplined, and no one showed an ounce of respect for Dr. Vata or the other group members. We spent more than a few sessions with someone locking him or herself in the bathroom, smashing a glass and cutting themselves with the shards. I wondered if the parents knew what was going on, and how disastrous the group sessions were. Dr. Vata never spoke to my mom and if I had told her what really went on in these sessions, she would never have believed me. I guess it was such early days for therapy that the parents did not have a clue as to what was supposed to go on, so they didn't challenge the doctor. I'm not sure what Dr. Vata's excuse was for the mess he was making in our young lives. He advised our parents not to interfere in the lives of their children, and they listened to him, with disastrous results. I took absolutely nothing helpful from those sessions and began to dread going back. I was witnessing the other group members becoming sicker. Just one example was that members were running away from home regularly. Everyone's grades were suffering. Some members were totally out of control and as a result my behavior became more and more out of control as well, both in and out of the group.

Prior to attending group therapy, I tried pot. I was about thirteen. I knew Joey from school. He was not much older than me, but certainly more experience with drugs. He rode up to me on his bike and pulled out this small baggy loaded with curly dark leaves that had a pungent and penetrating, unforgettable smell. The vegetation inside was cannabis. It was quite lousy quality, in that it was loaded with stems and seeds, but I didn't know any different, so was game. He just gave me the plastic baggy with the pot without asking for money, and I stuffed the plastic bag into my bra, hopped onto my bike and sped around the neighborhood showing off my new prize to my friends. It was amazing, I felt so elated, so daring, so grown up.

It was all wonderful, until I got down to the nitty gritty. The first time I tried to smoke it was a huge disappointment. Joey included a joint in the bag that he rolled, so I was ready to rock and roll. I struck a match from the pack I carried for cigarettes, and then puffed away on the joint for a full five minutes. Then I waited for that utopian moment, seventh heaven or at least something. I waited and waited. Ten minutes, twenty...nothing! I'd been conned, perhaps this was why they called it shit because that's what it was. Shit, pure shit. I felt cheated. I chatted with one of my hipper friends the next day and told him I had smoked my first joint. He was really happy for me and asked how it was. I lied, said it was great to save face.

That could have been the end except the following day somebody else came over to me, pulled me aside, and insisted I have another joint. Joey had run his mouth to everyone about the fact I got stoned, and now it seemed getting me stoned was a neighborhood project. It took a week before anything like a high came from smoking pot, but it finally did. I was pretty underwhelmed by my experience with pot. I knew that if I wanted to reliably change my mood I had to rely on pills. And so it went. I smoked some pot on occasion, but mostly I spent time finding sources for pills, mostly speed, which I took to feel better.

I had heard about a progressive school called Hawthorne, in southwest Washington D.C., and begged my parents to let me switch from public to private school. I made dozens of promises that I'd be good and fit in. Eventually I wore them down the said I could try attending classes there. On my first day, I went into the gym to hang out after the initial introduction was finished. There were two other people lounging on a large tumbling mat on the floor.

'Hi, my name is Jan and I just started school today.'

'Cool. My name is Kippy Tweedy...you like to get high?'

'Sure.' I was game and up for some fun, forgetting in an instant all the promises I'd made to my parents. Perhaps this place would be as amazing as I heard it was. The other girl didn't say much. Kippy was a visual treat, tall and lanky with flaming red, curly hair. He introduced me to the girl.

'This is Pam.'

'Nice to meet you.'

'Sure is,' she said. 'Let's smoke.' She pulled out a joint that was already rolled.

Kippy held up a lighter, lit the joint and Pam took a huge drag. It was then passed to me.

'Thanks.' I took a long pull on the joint and blew the smoke high up into the air.

Kippy reached out for his turn, took a drag…and a teacher walked in. We were busted. We sat there with the thick smoke cloud hovering above our heads. Shit!

We were marched down to the headmaster's office. Sandy and Eleanor Orr ran the school. They were extremely liberal and very wonderful. All three of us were questioned about what we had done. Kippy and I admitted that we had smoked pot, but Pam lied and swore she hadn't smoked it, protesting her innocence, and in the end they believed her. Kippy and I ended up getting suspended from school for a week. A great start at a new school for me, and Pam was never punished at all. I'm sure there was a lesson in there somewhere, but I didn't pick up on it. Nevertheless, despite my loathing for Pam at that moment, we would go on to become best friends for over fifty years (and counting). Having a best friend was great because I never really felt like I had one. I got quite close to a girl called Ellen Zaslow and was devastated when she moved to Japan. She was gone from the second to the fifth grade. We wrote to each other nearly every month while she was away. Many years later I heard that her father was in the CIA, which accounted for her moving but as a kid I knew nothing about that. I just really loved Ellen's parents and enjoyed spending time at her house playing with her.

I kept striving to find ways I could give of myself to feel better about myself. That was the only time I felt worthy and good. I started attending the youth group at the Unitarian Church. I was Jewish but was not involved with a temple. Pam was a Unitarian and I became curious about her religion as what she shared about it appealed to me. It was characterized by a free and responsible search for truth and meaning and I felt it was an organization I could explore and study with Pam. Unitarian Universalists do not share one specific religion or creed but are unified by their shared search. I was amazed to hear that the Unitarian Universalist Church included many agnostics, theists, and even atheists among its membership. It was hard to understand. Pam explained that that all its members had a deep regard for tolerance, intellectual freedom and inclusive love, so that its members could research and take knowledge, comfort and meaning from all religions of the world. I would give it a try.

I joined the Liberal Religious Youth, or LRY for a short time. We had meetings where we shared fellowship and I even got to make a presentation at a Sunday Service.

The most fulfilling part was to be involved in activities which the church sponsored, including a clean-up project in a poor black neighborhood near Bethesda, Maryland. We were told they had no trash services, but the authorities had promised that if the residents could clean up the garbage that littered their yards, they would be given a regular trash pick-up. We were dropped off on the outskirts of the neighborhood, armed with trash bags and gloves. I couldn't quite believe the depravation, squalor and sheer filth. The garbage was literally knee deep in places. These people had lost hope. How had it gotten this bad in an area that was only a few miles from where I lived, and not far from one of the poshest sections of Montgomery County, Maryland?

I thought the clean-up task was impossible, but we refused to be discouraged, so we plowed ahead. As we were clearing the top layer from the piles of rubbish the enormity of the task at times overwhelmed us. The stench was indescribable, and we uncovered rotting food and dirty diapers, car and motorcycle tires, pizza boxes and bits of rotting wood. More than once a large rat scrambled to safety from beneath the debris, bringing shrieks and screams from my fellow workers.

And yet, I was in heaven. I was knee deep in shit, quite literally, but I couldn't have been happier because I knew that I was making a difference and the reward at the end would make it all worthwhile. Our group labored all day and at times I seemed as if we were barely scratching the surface. Finally, at the end of the day when we finished, we were all so pleased with the results. The yards and the surrounding streets weren't perfect, but they were clean enough to have trash service in their neighborhood. I was so proud and so happy for the residents, and grateful that I could help.

Ultimately, I returned to my Jewish roots. Even though I enjoyed the youth activities, there was a deep resonance with my being and the Jewish religion and culture. As I got older, I realized I took a great deal of my identity from my Judaism. In later life it became my fondest dream to become a rabbi, a dream I have never abandoned, even though I am now seventy. You never know.

5

Starting at fifteen, I just couldn't help running away on a regular basis, at least once a month, and sometimes more. On the first occasion I ran away I'd had a huge fight with my parents. I took off and then decided it would be a good idea to see if I could get into a nightclub called Birdland, which was in a rough part of Washington, D.C. I wasn't very sophisticated about being in a bar. I lit up my cigarette and tried to act cool, leaving my purse unattended on the table, and surprise, surprise, it was stolen. My first reaction was to get up and leave but I realized that I was enjoying the music enough to stay. It wasn't long before I met a guy who wanted to sit with me. I felt grown up and wanted and enjoyed the attention he was paying to me. He offered to buy me a drink, but I declined. I didn't have a fake ID so I couldn't drink, but that didn't really matter because I never really liked booze that much anyway. I had smoked a joint earlier, so I was feeling pretty good and the music kept me in that mood. I told him about my stolen purse and complained I had no money to get home. He said that if I wanted to, I could come over and spend the night with him. That seemed a much better alternative than going home to my family and the inevitable fight, so I ended up staying out all night and a few more days after that. The guy wasn't all that special, but I thought I should sleep with him because he'd been nice enough to let me stay at his place and feed me.

Needless to say, I didn't really think that much of myself at this point. I had recently lost my virginity to a guy named Jerry. It was one of the most torturous, horrible experiences of my youth. I honestly don't remember where I met him, but he was in the Navy and said that he was going to be shipping out. I was fifteen and he was in his mid-twenties. He came over to visit me at my house two times. Both times my parents were home so things were pretty quiet. We just hung out and talked. On the third occasion however, he brought a friend with him and had a clear plan mapped out. I lived in a split-level home. He said he was getting ready to ship out the next day and insisted he cared for me so much that we had to cement our relationship in the only way possible and that was to have sex before he left. I refused at first, but his sweet-talking and over generous compliments had an effect on me. I do not remember how he twisted this whole thing around, but he said having sex with me was the one thing that would keep him loving me from so far away. He swore undying love and faith and loyalty and although I could smell the bullshit, part of me was so thrilled that someone was paying so much attention to me. Eventually I gave in to him and asked him how we would do it.

His friend was positioned at the top of the stairs, standing guard and watching out for my parents. Jerry and I went to the downstairs bathroom. He dropped his trousers and urged me to start stroking his penis which by this time was quite hard and getting stiffer by the second. He sat back on the toilet and beckoned me forward and told me sit on his penis. I had taken off my underpants, so I was bare under my dress, but trying to sit on him was almost an impossibility. It was too painful. He tried to push his penis into me while he sat there red-faced and moaning, but I kept pulling back. I wanted to scream but knew that my parents were just upstairs so I dared not make a noise. By now he had his hands firmly clenched on my buttocks as he forced me down on top of him while he thrust into me. My God, it was so damned awful, so painful and messy and not pleasurable in the slightest. Thankfully, it was all over very quickly. He pulled up his trousers with a big sickly grin plastered all over his face. I don't even know for sure if he ejaculated or not. The experience was horrible. I assume he got off.

It was the last time I ever saw him. It really left me with no special regard for sex, so that later when I stayed with the guy from Birdland, sleeping with him seemed a fair exchange for a place to stay for a few days. There was just nothing precious about it.

Though I wasn't locked up after my first time running away, in the future when I ran away again, my parents handed me over to the juvenile authorities. That meant I would spend time at a juvenile detention facility, Thomas J.S. Waxter's Children's Facility.

By the age of sixteen I began running away regularly from school, hanging out with the wrong crowd, smoking dope and taking drugs. When I ran away, I would usually find some guy to shack up with for a few days. I really did not have the means to stay out very long on my own and there was always an expected payment to the guys I stayed with. Every one of them eventually came on to me and I had no option but to give them my body. Sometimes the guys were cute and tender and loving, and I enjoyed the experience but that was rare. Most times I would just get sick of the guy and show up back home.

There would be the inevitable fights with my parents and then I would be placed in a juvenile detention facility. Sometimes they incarcerated me for up to a month. Detention was a miserable experience; the place was run like a prison. There were no individual cells. There were segregated single rooms for males and females and sometimes we were thrown together in a big dormitory, which again was segregated by male and female. Every morning boys and girls could all congregate in a communal area. The rules were strict, the time was spent miserably and the boredom at times was unbearable. I honestly do not remember many details, but I do recall the horrible blue wrap-around skirts we had to wear and the disgusting food. I was overweight and felt as if every boy was poking fun at me. We were all given a small ration of cigarettes (I bet that doesn't happen anymore). I was miserable, back to the point of suicide. I was always counting the days until my release. Once released, the cycle would start all over again. School, depression, pot and drugs, run away, sex with a stranger, back home, fights and incarceration.

All these behaviors were extremely troubling for my parents and they kept looking to Dr. Vata to somehow perform a miracle. Looking back now I see it was really a case of the blind leading the blind. Dr. Vata was clueless. There were no parental meetings, no explanations, no diagnosis and no subsequent cure and the young patients under his care became more fucked up by the day, me included. It was like one huge big veil of secrecy and silence. He told the parents nothing, and I honestly believe he had nothing to tell them.

I was forced to attend Dr. Vata's group therapy sessions until I was about seventeen. Little did I know how much of an impact the events that played out at the group would have on my life. More about that later.

The very first acid trip I took was on New Year's Eve when I was about seventeen years old. I was still at Hawthorne school and I was on a downward spiral. Drugs were my only solace. A girl had asked me to come out to her house and as I had nothing better to do, I decided to tag along with Pammy and some friends who were also invited. We went out to Middleburg, Virginia, to a sprawling estate. I couldn't believe the size of the mansion. The girl who gave the party had her father stashed in his game room. We peered in to see what he looked like and were blown away by his surroundings. Apparently, he had been a big game hunter, and had brought back trophies. The room in which he sat had the walls covered with animal heads, no doubt from those hunting trips. He was a shrunken up old guy who just sat staring into space in a huge easy chair, grinning inanely. He never opened his mouth and left everybody alone to carry on as they saw fit.

In another large room there were huge bowls of pills and some cocaine on a table and a big bowl of marijuana. Everything necessary to fuel the party and I couldn't wait to get loaded. I had heard all about the effects of acid and the spectacular hallucinations and I asked around the partygoers until someone eventually agreed to let me in on their acid stash.

A tall skinny guy opened his hand and grinned. 'Are you sure you are ready for this?'

There was a single piece of paper with a stamped psychedelic design in the palm of his hand. He handed the paper to me and I couldn't wait to put it into my mouth. I decided to suck on it for a while, figuring the drugs would break down quicker and hit my brain harder. Nothing remarkable happened over the next hour. I kept waiting for the instant 'bang' but apart from feeling a little lightheaded it was crap. I drank some soda and smoked some pot, but I didn't seem to be hallucinating at all. Where were the fireworks, the strange and wonderful things that were supposed to appear in front of me? I hung out at the party until the wee hours of the morning and then went to Pammy's house to sleep.

I lay down next to the Christmas tree and borrowed Pam's glasses which were extremely thick because she was blind as a bat. When I put on her glasses and looked at the colored lights on the Christmas tree, I had the sense that I was hallucinating. The lights were moving slightly, the colors a vivid contrast against the darkness of the branches of the tree. But then again, that effect could have been from the glasses that were incredibly thick. That seemed to be as good as it would get. So much for acid.

Amphetamines were my favorite. They really boosted my mood, taking me out of the darkness of my depression, if only for a little while. I finally found a reliable source. I had discovered Dr. Wheeler on Georgia Avenue in Wheaton Maryland. I think it was around $20 for an appointment to get the diet pills I craved. I tried to be cagey about being fat and wanting to lose weight. Then I would look at him sheepishly and ask for the amphetamines. I was careful not to go to him too often. He seemed happy to oblige me with prescriptions for Dexedrine. From time to time I asked him for some other types of pills like antibiotics, to make it seem like our relationship was legitimate, but it was the uppers that I was there for. I could do more, eat less, feel less depressed and just seemed to function better until the inevitable crash, which always happened. It seemed like I always had to increase the number of pills I took to achieve the same feeling, but because I could not go too often, there were times I was just out of pills and out of luck. Sometimes I would run out because I was taking them in greater numbers than were prescribed for me. During those times when I was out, I was so miserable. Once I got the new prescription all was well and I was happy again.

One day my father got a call from Detective Steve Filyo. I did not hear any of the call, but the next thing I knew my father was telling me to put on my coat and come with him. We drove to the police station in Silver Spring, Maryland. I had no idea what was going on. When we arrived, the detective took my father into another room and talked to him for about ten minutes. I remember looking at the closed door and wondered what the hell they were talking about. When my father came out, he walked straight up to me and slammed me in the head with a roundhouse. I was knocked halfway across the room.

The detective calmly pulled me aside into another room, leaving my father outside in the main reception area.

'What is going on?' I said. I was completely lost. I was hoping that the detective could give me some sort of an idea about what was happening.

Filyo looked at me and proceeded to explain. 'It seems that your girlfriend from your therapy group ran away from home. When she was finally found, she had some pot on her. She said she got the pot from you.'

'Are you crazy? Do you think I am going to take the blame for her pot?' I was dumbstruck but managed to continue. 'You don't understand,' I stuttered. 'I want to be a veterinarian and if I get busted for something like this it would ruin my chances of ever getting into school.'

The detective sat in silence shaking his head and at that moment my father came bursting into the room. He was holding my little green purse that he had confiscated just a few days before. It was a small purse, about twice the size of a fist. It seems that I had a habit of leaving it on the corner cabinet, just next to the front door in the living room. I kept the little green purse stuffed with bottles of the prescription drugs I got from Dr. Wheeler, and I mean *stuffed*. You could not miss the fact that the little purse was crammed with bottles. Later my parents would say it was my way of asking for help, leaving an obviously intriguing looking purse stuffed to the brim with something that begged investigation.

I couldn't think straight.

'If you can't get her on the marijuana, then you can get her on this,' my father said. He slammed my little green purse down on the table in front of Detective Filyo and walked out.

The detective let slip a small smile when he saw the contents. 'Okay, now we are talking about a serious legal problem with these bottles of pills as hard evidence. It's time for a confession.'

I was panicking because I knew that pills were way more dangerous than pot, but of course, this had nothing to do with their legal status. Back in 1967, marijuana was still adjudicated under the Harrison Narcotic Act, that is, it was treated like a narcotic, like heroin, and the punishments were comparable. What I did not know at the time was that my pills were totally legal for me to possess, a doctor had written me a prescription, so they were fine. It did not matter that I felt I had manipulated the doctor. That was just my guilt taking over.

Detective Filyo told me to come clean on supplying the pot and he would forget about the pills. If I didn't cooperate, he'd do his best to bust me any way he could. I looked at the four bottles of pills piled up on the table and knew I had to think fast. I was feeling sick, gripped with fear. The detective smiled as he fiddled with one of the bottles, passing it from one hand to the other.

Finally, I agreed to cop to the pot.

I signed a piece of paper as he informed me that my case would proceed before a judge. I don't know what was on the piece of paper; I couldn't see the writing for the tears that poured down my face. Not only had my father hit me but he had walked out of the room at the time I needed him the most. My face was throbbing and painful and I felt alone and deserted.

The other legal quirk at the time was that juveniles were not protected yet by the re Gault decision that gave them rights in court. That landmark decision came in one month after I was busted.

In re Gault 387 in 1967 was a Supreme Court decision that stated that juveniles accused of crimes in a delinquency proceeding must be afforded the same rights as adults, such as the right to timely notification of the charges, the right to confront witnesses, the right against self-incrimination and the right to counsel. The court's opinion was written by Judge Abe Fortas, a champion of children's human rights. Before then, the juvenile court system was run on the premise, 'Father Knows Best', that is, the judge, a supposed fatherly figure, would hand out his sentences guided by so-called fatherly wisdom and a desire to do what was best for the juvenile. In fact, it was a nothing more than a kangaroo court and young juvenile's rights were trampled on.

Thankfully, I was not taken into custody and was allowed to leave with my father. I am sure he felt confused and at least a little guilty about hitting me, though he never regretted siding with the law against me. We didn't talk for quite a while

All too quickly my case came around and I found myself sitting in the courtroom facing Judge Alfred D. Noyes. The judge was silent most of the hearing. Finally, he spoke. He looked across the bench sternly. I will never forget his words when he passed sentence.

'I am sentencing you to a period of incarceration at a psychiatric hospital.'

I looked at my father who sat in the court room. He didn't react.

Judge Noyes continued. 'Don't think of this time as punitive. Instead think of it as rehabilitative. And don't think of your stay in terms of days. Think more in terms of months.'

I would be in there for ten months.

I couldn't quite take it in. Locked up. How long for, I wondered. I tried to ask him, but I was ignored and shuttled out of the courtroom. This was when I was introduced to the social worker from Jewish Family Services, Coy Patrick. My mother had contacted them, asking for their help in my case. Coy introduced herself and explained that she would drive me over to the hospital and see that I was settled. She was a pleasant looking middle-aged woman, with brownish, blondish curly hair, and a gentle round face.

'No way is she Jewish,' I thought.

So, there I was, seventeen years old and about to enter Springfield State Psychiatric Hospital in Sykesville, MD. The judge had sentenced me to a snake pit. *The Snake Pit* was the title of a 1948 movie I saw, which portrayed a crazy woman played by Olivia de Havilland during her long stay in a mental institution. The scenes in the movie came flooding back to me, the men in the white coats, Olivia de Havilland screaming that she was tormented and confused. I was terrified.

Looking back I have come to understand what a devastating decision this was. The system had stupidly set me up for the destruction of my young psyche. At seventeen, juveniles are striving to develop an identity. They do this in part by looking to the people in their environment and learning by emulating the behavior they observe. The environment I would learn from consisted of crazy patients, junkies, and psychotic staff. The experience also created a war that raged inside of me for many years, where I was pitted against society's idea of who they thought I was. It left me with no trust of our system of 'justice'. This experience created a terrible internal struggle that lasted a great deal of my life. It took many years of hard work in therapy to soothe the pain of self-hatred that was driven into me from these experiences. It is extremely hard to fight against institutional injustice. When that fight takes place in your head, there is always psychic damage, self-condemnation. The damage is never fully repaired, and I would forever walk with a psychological limp. It was terrifying from the first moment.

When I first arrived in Ward D in the L building, I thought I had died and gone to hell. I will never forget this thirtysomething black woman, a patient, with a short blonde Afro, hospital gown flapping open in the back, revealing her buttocks. She was walking in circles screaming that she was Jesus Christ. She screamed at the top of her voice. I was absolutely petrified. (Some weeks later, she got to move on to a higher ward with more privileges and I was still sitting in Ward D. Because I was court ordered I was stuck on a lower ward with the sicker patients. This only served to make me feel terrible.)

I could only think about leaving. When I would ask one of the nurses how long I would be here, they would shrug their shoulders, and say, 'No one knows my dear.'

And so, from that first night at seventeen years of age, when they locked me in a secure ward, I would awake around midnight, screaming my lungs out. Every night after that, until well after I left the hospital, I would continue having night terrors, screaming myself awake.

My time in Springfield was crazy. My friends were mostly junkies that came in from Baltimore to take a thirty-day heroin detox. The other inmates were generally too crazy to get close to. I'd try to talk to some of them but from the outset it was clear they were on another planet. The junkies were definitely the easiest to relate to. We would sit around playing Tonk or Wisp, card betting games where you could win or lose cigarettes, candy bars or smuggled medications. Patients would pretend to swallow their meds and save them for barter. Money was useless, but cigarettes, pills and candy bars were the coin of the realm. It was nothing to swap pills for a candy bar, a fact I often lamented when I was back on the streets being hit up for a lot of money when I was making a drug purchase.

The biggest frustration was not knowing how long I was going to be in there. If they had told me, I think I could have handled it. I would have accepted my punishment, knuckled down and counted off the days, but no matter who I asked, even my parents, all I got was a blank look or a shrug of the shoulders.

The whole time there I was kept on a lower ward. Having been prevented to move to upper wards, I lost out on greater freedom and more privileges. I was never allowed to have matches, or sharps. My possessions were closely monitored.

One particularly bad time I got in trouble for a prank I pulled off with my friend Wendy. Wendy was my age and in because she was suicidal. She had a ton of freckles and was always wearing flowered muumuus.

The two of us managed to get in trouble constantly. Anything for a giggle. We used to write *Sykesville* as the return address on any letters we sent home. This didn't go down too well with the staff, but it wasn't far from the truth.

When we pulled off our big prank it just seemed like a harmless gag, something to lighten up the tediousness of the day. Wendy had just gotten back from being sent to a lower ward as a punishment. The threat of being sent to a lower ward was scary. They were totally restrictive, you could only eat with a spoon - no knives and forks for obvious reasons - and the cigarettes were handed out two at a time, four times a day. You were allowed almost no possessions and you were locked in the day room, a large room with a television blaring in the corner the whole day. As bad as D was, the lowest ward was worse. It was where they housed the most violent patients, and the danger when you were there was real.

The hospital just had new signs painted on many of the doors. A man had come in and carefully hand-lettered signs on the door, *Bathroom*, *Office*, and more. We thought it would be funny to scratch off some of the letters to alter the signs and we waited until the corridor was clear. We began our task, giggling like two schoolgirls. We scratched off some of the lettering to change the meaning, so the *Bathroom* became the *Bat room* and *Office* became *Off*, while an *X-ray Room* became *X Room*. It wasn't even particularly funny, but we still got a charge out of it. Unfortunately, at the wrong moment someone appeared, and we were caught!

We caught hell, but only I was banished to the lower ward.

I was terrified.

I begged with the nurses to spare me, but my pleas fell on deaf ears. I was doomed.

I spent ten days in a place that was how I imagine hell must be. I thought Ward D was bad. This place made it look like heaven.

I sit all alone
By ward telephone
It rings but not for me

Corner tv plays
Gameshow dramas all day
Pleasure melting away from my days
In my backward world raped emotions are hurled
And my tranquilizers eat me
Stifled screams choke my soul
Drugs deaden this hole
Mind and soul are buried with dreams

And I sit by the phone
As the time passes on
Just my ashtray betrays the hours I've stayed
Tiled walls echo shrieks
And nobody speaks
'Cept to say hello
On ward telephone

When I first entered the punishment ward I was petrified. I crawled under a large table and tried to go to sleep. The noise from arguments between staff and patients, and patients shouting at patients was too much to bear. Hiding under the table didn't help so I moved. No more than five minutes after I moved from under the table to a chair, a fight broke out and the table I had been lying under was overturned. If I had not moved I would have been crushed. As two inmates punched and scratched each other, they fell onto the table, which collapsed. Immediately the nurses descended on the altercation, restoring order with their own brand of mayhem. They waded in with punches and slaps and expertly executed restraining holds. The nurses looked like they had been recruited from a wrestling team. They were huge and not averse to violence. In fact, if anything, I believed they secretly enjoyed a little violence to break the monotony of the day. On more than one occasion I saw a nurse pick up a patient using a chokehold on the neck. She held her forearm under the patient's chin and transported her across the floor with the rest of the body dangling. It seemed acceptable practice to restrain the more violent patients any way they wanted to, and with even the slightest provocation. Any excuse seemed to justify patient abuse.

The lower wards were unbelievably frightening. Everyone seemed out of control. The level of violence was sickening and seemed to manifest in horrific behavior. It was as if the toxicity mutated into different sick expressions. Self-mutilation became a group sport among the patients. They would compete to see who could garner the most attention by creating new and more horrific ways to do self-harm. Mostly they would either scratch themselves or swallow things. Often, they would pull magazines apart to get the staples, which they would swallow. Sometimes they would swallow pennies, or any tiny object they could get down their throats. They loved the fuss that was made when they were x-rayed. I'm sure most were starved for attention and settled for it at any cost. Witnessing the patients' self-destructive antics really cast a dim light on my own attempts in the past at self-mutilation. After a few tragic breakups, I had scratched the guy's name on my arm with a bobby pin. Witnessing the others' lunacy took all the fun out of that behavior, so I stopped it. It's amazing how much insight one gains when you see someone else performing your loony behavior.

6

After a month in Springfield, I had an important visitor. I was sitting in the room where we did occupational therapy. Basically, we were given simple and cheap arts and crafts material to fill our time making things. A member of staff told me that they were no longer allowed to have patients weave baskets because of the negative association with the mentally ill. It had been common practice in mental institutions for many years, dating back to the nineteenth century. But now basket-weaving was viewed as a lowly activity, childlike, feminine, and potentially dehumanizing. The use of the term 'basket case' was a very common expression to describe someone of very low intelligence and anyone displaying lunatic-like traits.

So, I was sitting with my latest project and looked down the hall when I saw a man. He was medium height, stocky and dressed in a dark suit. His walk was distinctive. He bounced on his heels as he headed down the hallway, walking directly towards me as if he knew me. As he got closer, I could see he wore thick black glasses and sported a nice black hat. All in all, he made a very dignified impression.

He walked straight up to me and said,

'You must be Jan. My name is Rabbi Eugene Lipman. Your mother asked me to come and visit you.'

This would be the beginning of a relationship that, in combination with my psychoanalyst, Dr. Herman Meyersburg, would save my life. (My work with Dr Meyersburg would come almost twenty years later.)

Rabbi Lipman visited me every month, even enduring a travel time that was easily two hours long. I felt he believed in me from the very first time we met. He encouraged me to think about spending time in Israel and even think about living there someday. Rabbi gave me a sense of hope for my future. He made me feel like a worthwhile human being instead of a throwaway.

Passover was coming soon, and I decided I would honor the holiday. Passover was always a very special experience for me. I really enjoyed having the ceremonial meal, called the Seder, and the general fun and laughter with my friends and family. Even though being in hospital left me completely remote from all of that, I still wanted to do something special to console me. I decided to create my own Seder. The Seder incorporates telling the story of the liberation of the Israelites from slavery in Egypt and the toughest part of pulling this off was that I did not read Hebrew. However, I knew that since

Rabbi Lipman would be visiting me, he could teach me what I needed to know. I wouldn't be able to do anything elaborate but whatever I could do would mean a lot to me. I would give myself an A for effort! And so, Rabbi Lipman taught me how to pronounce the different letters of the Hebrew alphabet. While I could've read an alliteration, which is a phonetic spelling of the Hebrew words, I really wanted to be able to read from the Hebrew text. I was able to talk to the staff about getting a few items of food that would represent the traditional Jewish foods. Certain foods were needed at the Seder to represent parts of the epic story. Salt water represents tears. That was easy. Hard-boiled eggs, which represents spring and the circle of life, were no problem either. Bitter herbs, representing the bitterness of slavery, came easy too as we used parsley. The roasted lamb bone, representing the Passover sacrifice, was substituted with a chicken bone. Finally, the *haroset*, which stood for the sweetness of life, was simply applesauce. The rabbi was kind enough to provide the *matzah*, the unleavened bread, and the kitchen gave us extra food for the feast.

Rabbi Lipman visited me regularly during the run-up to Passover and I diligently practiced pronouncing Hebrew to the best of my ability. The kitchen staff were great and more than helpful assisting with something that they sensed meant a great deal to me. We put together a small feast. When it came time to have the Seder everyone who had helped, or just happened to be there, joined in. I had to abbreviate the ceremony as everyone seemed impatient to finish. I understood. They weren't Jewish and it really made no sense, but I made them wait a little while and we all did the best we could. I knew that no one could really tell if I was getting it right, so I wasn't nervous. I just pushed my way through it. Ultimately, we had a great time and a nice meal. I believe everyone enjoyed it. As I started eating, I was feeling pretty good about myself and even though we skipped a lot of the ceremony it still gave me a sense of the occasion. I felt good about myself. That night I slept well. For the first time in a long while I felt I had gotten a piece of my Jewish identity back.

By the end of the week the Passover celebration was a distant memory and once again I was faced with the reality that I was locked in a secure ward in a psychiatric hospital, night after night, and with no date of release.

I hit the bottom with no end in sight.

Time after time I'd ask the staff when I'd be going home. They said the biggest problem with getting me released was that no facility wanted to take me. I was considered dangerous. What the fuck!? Dangerous? They couldn't be serious. I'd passed some pot to a friend; I did not run amok with a machete slicing up the local population. The staff explained that marijuana had a dangerous reputation and most places did not want to be bothered with me.

There was a place called George's Junior Republic, in New England, and I was told that Coy had written to them. It was sort of a co-ed Boys Town and after several days we had a reply. I bounced into the office convinced I was on my way. Coy was there, with bad news. Boys Town wanted nothing to do with me.

Coy seemed to be trying very hard to find somewhere that would take me and after ten long months, she finally had good news for me. They were looking at releasing me through a new special program Jewish Social Services that had just started. It was a foster program. Juveniles in trouble could live with a caring family and hopefully the experience would give the juvenile a chance to heal and live well. I was all for it. Mostly I just wanted to get the hell out of Springfield.

Though I believe Jewish Social Services had the right motives when they created the foster program, either they did not have the sophistication to oversee it properly, or I was just extremely unlucky.

7

My first foster placement was with a remarkably interesting family; the Sagans.

Dr. Leonard Sagan was a nuclear physician working for the Atomic Energy Commission. I did not really understand what he did, but he was different from a nuclear physicist. He was interested in the health of the body, and the rest would only be a guess. Mrs. Sagan was a tiny woman with black hair which she wore in the pixie style. She always had a sweet smile and spoke with a French accent. Most notably, she was a gourmet cooking teacher. Because of her classes, we had the most wonderful food imaginable. I still regret that I did not learn more cooking skills from her. I am sure she would have loved to teach me, as her two boys had no interest in developing culinary skills.

During the time I stayed with the Sagans their boys were eight and ten years old. The family lived in a large house in suburban Rockville, Maryland. The beautiful white frame house sat on a corner lot with plenty of trees. I had a lovely little bedroom to myself and my first impression was totally positive. However, their lifestyle and mine did not mesh very well, and from the beginning I thought that would be a problem.

Madame Sagan's cooking class seemed to have no shortage of women eager to learn from her. These were very wealthy society ladies, many of whom arrived in chauffeur-driven cars. I was very anti-establishment at the time, especially after my recent experience in Springfield, so seeing these wealthy women irritated me.

I really didn't have many friends, but I did meet some other hippie types who hung around in Rockville. We smoked dope and drank wine when we got together, and we always talked politics. We were all very much against the government's position on Vietnam. We felt it was a civil war that America had no right to be involved in.

I attended high school at night so I could graduate. One night I got into a huge argument with a girl whose brother was fighting in Vietnam. I said I absolutely thought the war was wrong and she said I should go to hell and that I was unpatriotic. I knew her brother was in Vietnam and understood why she was so upset, but I stayed with my belief that we shouldn't be there. At one point we were nose-to-nose, shouting at each other. I really did not want to back down. The argument was stopped by the teacher. We never agreed with each other, but the pointlessness of continuing the fight became apparent, so we stopped. I never shared these difficulties with my foster parents but kept everything bottled up inside.

My dismal social life had a bright spot for a short period of time when I met Scotty Wilkerson. Like me, he was a bit of an outcast, a misfit. We truly loved each other. He was the first guy who paid serious attention to me and liked me for who I was. He wasn't tall, just my height, with a little boy's body that was muscular. He had a pixie-shaped face, turned up nose and a ready smile. I was still fighting depression at the time and Scotty helped me a lot. He gave me confidence and genuinely seemed to enjoy being around me. I loved that.

But my demons still battled me from the inside. I began arguing with him for no apparent reason, almost picking fights with him just to see how far I could push him. It was as if I were testing him to find out just how much he would put up with. Eventually I went too far and pushed him away. We stopped dating. This testing of others seemed to happen a lot, and I managed to push many people out of my life, even when I liked them.

I never stopped loving Scotty, even though I stopped seeing him. Then I heard that he was killed in a car crash. I learned about his death months after his funeral. I wasn't given any details, and, quite honestly, I didn't want to hear them anyway. I was told that there was a group of his friends on motorcycles that led the funeral procession. I know Scotty would have loved that.

The news of Scotty's death pushed me deeper into my depression.

Life became unbearable. I could not get out of bed unless it was completely unavoidable.

I tried extremely hard to have some common ground with Madame Sagan. She wanted to cheer me up and was kind enough to cater a wonderful birthday party for me and my friends. I felt guilty since I knew I had done nothing to deserve her kindness. I pushed myself to try to spend some time with her. Even though I was not getting close to her, I couldn't help liking and admiring her. She was truly an agent for peace and the stories she told me were fascinating. I knew in my heart she was a special person. During World War II she risked her life in the underground movement and was awarded a medal from the Italian Government for bravery. I've since researched that her medal was one of only seven medals that were given by the Italian senate. The stories Madame Sagan told me were thrilling. She described how she performed acts of true heroism, but she was always very modest in the retelling. I had to push her for details, and I could see it was painful for her to relive the more harrowing moments, even when the stories ended in personal victory. She never told me about the darkest of her struggle with the Nazis. That was something I found out much later in life, long after Ginetta Sagan had passed away. At the time I did not know how big a heroine, a fighter, a campaigner for human rights and a workhorse for Amnesty International she was. She performed many acts of heroism, risking her life with no thought to her peril. She was responsible for bringing Amnesty International to North America late in life. Amnesty International has honored her with a special award in her name.

One amazing story I shall never forget is when she freed an entire train car filled with prisoners. World War II had created an Italian civil war of its own, with a complex framework of politics influenced by external factors, including fascism and the Nazis. In 1943 Benito Mussolini was ousted and arrested by order of the king, which provoked civil war. The northern half of the country was occupied by 600,000 German soldiers. The south was governed by monarchist and liberal forces, who fought for the Allied cause and to free the north from German occupation. Any Italians in the north who refused to side with the Germans were made prisoner and taken away to the many POW camps in Italy, or even transported as slave labor internees to Germany. Madame Sagan never told me exactly where the train was, but it was undoubtedly en route to Germany. It just so happened that the train was passing close to where she lived, and she organized some food parcels at one of the stations. She laughed as she told me the Nazi guards didn't seem to object to her presence and they actually flirted with the smiling Italian girls and young mothers. Also, feeding the prisoners would make them stronger and they'd work longer and harder when they eventually arrived at their destination. They only checked the first few food parcels Ginetta passed through the carriage window. The last few bundles contained metal files that the prisoners used to break their steel bindings. The train parked in a siding for the night, just a few miles from the Austrian border and most of the German guards slept soundly, safe in the knowledge that every prisoner was chained to an iron rail that ran the length of the carriage. In the early hours of the morning, every single prisoner made good their escape and disappeared into the darkness of the Italian countryside. Madame Sagan laughed as she told me how much she would have loved to have seen the Nazi faces when they opened the carriages in the morning.

On another occasion she relayed more harrowing tales about occasions when she would be carrying a backpack with radio equipment that she was trying to smuggle past the Nazis, only to be stopped at a checkpoint. When they asked her what she was carrying, she feared the worst but bluffed her way through and said she just had some bread and offered to give them some. If they had taken her up on her offer she would have been caught and killed, as they would have realized that the backpack contained radio equipment that was destined for the Resistance. She succeeded every time. She believed that her tiny stature and her young, innocent face were what saved her.

Madame Sagan was finally caught towards the end of the war. She said that if the war had continued longer, she would have died. She was imprisoned and tortured. She would not go into detail, but she did share that the Nazis broke both of her wrists which was why she had problems holding heavy pans. She once showed me a scar on her neck where she was grazed by a bullet. I had the feeling that she suffered sexual abuse, but she did not confide the worst of her experiences to me.

Madame Sagan was not upset when she spoke about what happened, not even when she spoke of the torture. I am so sorry that I cannot turn back the clock and tell her how wonderful she was, based on what I know now. I was a sullen, depressed teenager, sadly stuck in my own misery, which left me incapable of fully appreciating her. That came later.

I looked into her story when I was much older. Allow me to share what I learned: Ginetta was born in Milan, her father was Catholic and her mother Jewish. Her parents were well aware of the rising anti-Semitism in Europe and arranged false papers, identifying her as Christian in order to hide her Jewish roots.

When World War II began, both of her parents became active in the Italian resistance movement, opposing fascist rule, only to be arrested in 1943 by Mussolini's Black Brigade. Her father was executed and her mother sent to Auschwitz, where she died in the gas chambers. Ginetta, just seventeen years old, was already active in the resistance movement, delivering food coupons and clothing to Jews who were in hiding. After her parents' death she became more heavily involved and started working as a courier for resistance forces in Northern Italy, as well as helping to print and distribute anti-government pamphlets. Fear was something that never seemed to trouble her and on one occasion she dressed as a cleaning lady to steal letterheads from government offices, to be used to forge letters of safe passage to Switzerland. Her daring and secret exploits were the stuff of legend and, since she was only five feet tall, she acquired the nickname *Topolino*. Little Mouse.

The war was ending but in late February 1945 Ginetta was betrayed by an informer and arrested by the Black Brigade. She was kept in prison for more than forty days and was beaten, raped and tortured before being told that she had been found guilty and would be executed. On the day of her scheduled execution she was taken to a villa in Sondrio, Italy, when a pair of German officers forced her Italian captors to release her into their custody. She later recalled watching the stars from the window of their car, whispering quietly, 'I will never see another dawn'. However, the Germans revealed themselves to be Nazi defectors who were collaborating with her resistance comrades and they delivered her safely to a Catholic hospital. Madame Sagan celebrated that day, April 23rd, for the rest of life. Such an amazing history. I'm sorry I did not have a better relationship with her. She passed from cancer some time ago, and I guess I will have to wait to tell her how much I admire her when I see her on the other side.

Most of my time at the Sagans was spent sleeping. I was still depressed and found myself sleeping my days away. I wanted to get close to the family, especially Madame Sagan, but always felt that I was somehow kept at arm's length. I was very much alone. I can't recall too many conversations with Dr. Sagan but do recall that he told the odd naughty joke. They weren't particularly funny, except one that I remember: Two women were waiting to get a picture taken by a professional photographer. The photographer goes over to the camera, fix it on a tripod and proceeds to fiddle with the dials on the camera. One woman turns to the other and says, 'What's he trying to do?' 'I think he's trying to focus,' comes the answer, to which the first woman responds, 'Both of us?'

Maybe you had to be there...

I knew that peace was important to Madame Sagan, but we never discussed anything about her feelings about the war in Vietnam. She had no idea that I cared. In fact, it was while I was staying at the Sagans that I went to the demonstration against the war in Vietnam, at the Pentagon, where my picture would be taken by Marc Riboud.

I made a conscious decision to get involved with the anti-war movement and have my feelings heard. There were protests going on all over the country and I needed to get involved. Perhaps this was exactly the sort of therapy I needed.

Normally I slept my days away, but this day was special. I'd never been to a demonstration before, so I really didn't know what to expect but I was excited at the prospect of meeting other hippies like myself. It was rumored that the demonstrators could number in the thousands and I'd heard the Yippies were going to be there with their flag. They could be relied upon to bring some good dope. I couldn't wait to see the Yippies, in particular Abbie Hoffman and Jerry Rubin, who were the leaders of the group. The Yippies were frequently seen at anti-war demonstrations with dozens of their flags, which had a black background with a five-pointed red star in the center and a green cannabis leaf superimposed over it. Once, when asked about the Yippie flag, an anonymous Yippie told the *New York Times*, 'The black is for anarchy, the red star is for our five point program and the leaf is for marijuana, which is how we get ecologically stoned without polluting the environment.' I loved that story; it was everything I admired their movement for.

This day was important for me and I couldn't imagine what to wear. I had almost no clothes I felt good in. I was overweight and everything just made me look fat. I decided to wear my pink paisley shift dress as it seemed to kind of hide my stomach. I put on my watch with the thick leather band I tooled myself, pulled on my knee-high brown leather boots and I was ready.

I hadn't said anything to the Sagans about attending the demonstration. I knew they believed in peace but I was afraid they might stop me. I really didn't want them interfering or getting worried, so I waited until after breakfast and slipped out the back door. I grabbed some money for my bus fare and walked over to where the D.C. transit bus would stop and take me down to Washington, D.C.

As I got closer to the heart of Washington, I saw more and more groups of people along the way. There were literally thousands of demonstrators including radicals, liberals, black nationalists, hippies, professors, women's groups, and war veterans all marching towards the Pentagon. I saw groups of people walking together, carrying placards and banners. I was amazed because I only expected the people to look like me, a bunch of hippies. I was completely shocked when I saw mothers pushing baby carriages, nuns and priests and other people who looked middle-class and normal. There was a complete array of straight people.

I loved every minute of that day. As I got close to the monument, I got off the bus and looked around. I was hoping I was going to see some people I could hang out with. I wanted to mingle with people in the crowd, but ultimately felt too awkward to speak to anyone. As we converged on the Washington Monument, we all gathered around the reflecting pool. There were speakers blasting but I was completely oblivious to what was being said. Mostly, I was just blown away at the immense size of the crowd.

At some sort of signal, we all started walking towards the 14th St. Bridge and the Pentagon. I saw a group of young people carrying banners that said *Youth Against Fascism* and I decided to join them. I couldn't argue with that slogan. I marched in step with them and imitated what they were saying, 'Viva Che! Viva Che!', even though I didn't have the vaguest idea of who or even what a Che was! (Later that week I attended a meeting of this group. They turned out to be a pro-Palestinian group intent on the destruction of Israel. When one of them started to chant 'Death to the Jews!', I knew I was in the wrong place.)

So, we marched and we chanted and we sang. It was an incredible gathering of people who simply wanted to stop the fighting and the suffering of the Vietnamese people.

Before we got to the Pentagon, I threw myself down on the ground spontaneously and started singing 'God bless America'. I don't know why. I hadn't planned to do it but I just felt so moved by the moment as the energy of the march carried me along. I picked myself up, and continued to walk, passing a young girl handing out pale pink chrysanthemums. I accepted one and kept walking.

Some years later, I was interviewed by a journalist who was very curious about the type of flower I held.

'Is that one of the daisies the New York Fugs dropped?'

I had no idea. It seems the New York punk rock band called the Fugs, formed by Ed Sanders, Tuli Kupferberg, and Ken Weaver, had wanted to drop thousands of daisies over the Pentagon. It was no more than a publicity stunt; I mean, imagine being able to penetrate the air space over the Pentagon.

When it became apparent they could not drop the daisies they already purchased, they ended up handing them out in masses at the demonstration. In fact, those daisies may have appeared in another famous photo from that day. The picture of George Harris stuffing flowers into the gun barrels might be those same daisies. Sadly, George died some years ago, and we will never hear the story of where he got his flowers.

The whole time I was at the demonstration I was filled with a sense of purpose. I realized that what I was involved in was big and important and I was so pleased to be a part of it. For the first time ever I felt that I belonged to something important. Almost all of my life felt like shit, but this gave it meaning. I was marching and demonstrating for peace and that meant a lot to me. I was so glad that I was joining in with my fellow demonstrators to let our government know that we did not support the aggression against the Vietnamese people.

As I walked a vision came to me, I clearly remembered a book from my younger days called the *Family of Man*. It featured pictures of all different races and nationalities and it helped me understand and see the diversity in people. I knew the Vietnamese people looked nothing like us, I could see that from the TV newsreels, but I understood that they were my brothers and sisters, that we are all part of the Family of Man.

As we marched towards the Pentagon, a line of soldiers stopped our progress. The national guard lined up in front of us with their rifles outstretched to prevent us from breaching the walls of the Pentagon. When I faced off with them, I did everything I could think of to get their attention or shake loose a reaction. I asked them to throw down their guns and join us. I started screaming at them, calling them baby killers and pawns of the war machine. They stared straight through me; a total stonewall. They never made eye contact, never made any connection with me. Marc Riboud later told me he observed them shaking. He thought they were probably afraid of getting an order to shoot, because we were being so provocative. Some years later I heard from another soldier who was in a different part of the demonstration, that they were shaking from the cold. It is my hope that someday I could meet the soldiers photographed with me so we could share our experiences and I have my questions answered.

Suddenly a huge floodlight came on. I thought it was for some kind of TV camera crew or something I could only imagine. I didn't let it faze me and continued as if they were not there.

I am not sure exactly when Marc Riboud photographed me. I know he captured me with the last of his film and the last light of the day. What was wonderful and not known by many, is that he captured me in a magical moment.

While I was holding the flower and looking at the soldiers, focusing on their young faces, in an instant it dawned on me. The rhetoric of the war machine and the baby killers completely melted away and suddenly I realized that these soldiers were just young boys. They could've been my brother, my cousin, my date. Sorrow swept right through me and I started to pity them. I held out the chrysanthemum in front of me. I held it with both hands, almost like a gesture of prayer. I became so very, very sad. These boys were just as much victims of this whole mess as anyone else. I became one with the soldiers. It was a moment of simpatico. At that very moment Marc Riboud's camera clicked and I became a part of history. It was 21 October 1967.

That shot was the last shot of the last roll of film with the last light of the day and then it was all over as darkness rolled in and we all drifted away. It had been a long day and I was exhausted. I didn't have far to walk to catch a bus back to the suburbs. I arrived at home, snuck in the back door, went quietly upstairs. It seemed that nobody had missed me. They probably assumed that I was asleep. Nothing was mentioned, as if my absence went unnoticed.

Months later, the night of my seventeenth birthday, we were having dinner when Madame Sagan handed me an envelope. 'Open it,' she urged.

I stared at the large manila envelope, clueless as to what it could contain. I slowly took out the contents. It was an 8x11 photo of me and a soldier, taken at the 1967 march against the war in Vietnam. I turned the photo over, and it said 'National Geographic Magazine' on the back along with the name of the photographer. I turned the paper over to study the image. Another demonstrator and me were on either side of a soldier, holding a long stick. We faced the camera. The soldier had his back to the camera. The stick balanced out the picture; I was kneeling on one side and an angry demonstrator facing the camera stood on the other side of the soldier with his fists clenched. It was an interesting study in contrast. My peaceful pose kneeling on one side, contrasted with the angry fist-clenching demonstrator standing on the other end of the stick. The soldier created a fulcrum, balancing the image on each side.

Madame Sagan was beaming. 'We were taking out-of-town guests to the Whitehouse Photography exhibit at the Library of Congress and what a surprise when I recognized you in the photograph. You can imagine that the last place we expected to see you was at the demonstration. We had no idea you went.' She continued as she reached across for the photo and studied it again. 'I wrote to the photographer at the *National Geographic* and he sent me this copy. We wanted you to have it.'

I was touched. Rather than punishing me for sneaking away to join the march, I think they were actually proud that I had gone. Madame Sagan was also a dedicated peace pilgrim. She risked her life for peace during World War II, which was far more than I felt I did. In fact, it was not until many years later that I realized how close I had come to death. It was only a few years after the march that the four students were killed at a demonstration at Kent State. While it is true that I felt protected because I was an American student, I naively thought that I was untouchable and that the only killing that could happen was taking place 9000 miles away. I was touched by what Madame Sagan did and wanted to pay her back in some way. I asked her whether I could get involved with Amnesty International, which she was involved with. She said she would be happy to have my help. 'As you know we've been very vocal about what's going on in Greece with the junta and how they are treating their political prisoners.'

In truth, I didn't know anything about it.

She told me about a letter that had appeared in the *Washington Post*. It was a letter to the editor from a man who claimed to be just a regular U.S. citizen who had recently visited Greece. He went on about what a wonderful democracy Greece had, claiming her citizens enjoyed a true democracy. Madame Sagan knew there was a huge problem, as she was sure this man had financial ties to the Greek government that were not disclosed. It was my job to find out whether he had a vested interest in the situation in Greece.

It turned out to be a relatively simple task. All people working on behalf of foreign governments must register as a foreign agent. I cross-referenced his name with the registered agents and, bingo, there he was.

A simple letter to the *Washington Post*, explaining that the man who wrote the letter praising the Greek junta was, in fact, on their payroll which obviously influenced his opinion, and the truth was out.

It was sensational. Madame Sagan exploited the obvious conflict of interest and the *Washington Post* printed a large article, explaining the role of Greek junta in suppressing freedom. Madame Sagan was delighted with me, but that would turn to hurt soon enough.

8

I had been there around six months when Madame Sagan pulled me aside and told me that she wanted to have a serious talk with me. She was very solemn and I even detected a little anger in her tone. Great. What have I done now?

'Jan,' she began, 'we understand that you are having great difficulty getting along here.'

Boy was that an understatement, I thought to myself.

'You are putting out sexual signals to Dr. Sagan and we are very concerned that you are trying seduce him.'

'What?'

At first I was speechless. Madame Sagan hadn't exactly beat about the bush with some polite small talk and she took me completely by surprise. It was almost laughable if it wasn't so hurtful.

The only thing I could think of was the way he looked, his crooked teeth when he smiled and his stubbly beard and grey hair. He was old compared to me, and there was no way I wanted anything to do with him sexually.

'You have to be kidding me?' I wailed.

Madame Sagan was serious.

I should have stayed there and argued my case, it would have only taken a few minutes to convince her that her husband was quite safe. But I didn't. Instead I screamed that she should leave me alone and ran up to my room where I locked myself in.

It took a few days for this to come to a head and the next thing I knew I was being transferred to another foster family. I was only too happy to go as I felt so hurt by her and couldn't wait to get out of there. I felt completely let down, particularly by Doctor Sagan's crazy accusation.

It was clear I had no defense, but at least a new home would give me another chance.

What has become a true source of regret is that I never met with Ginetta Sagan again. Only years later did I find out more about her life and what a truly great person I'd shared a home with, if only for a few months and with a good deal of emotional distance.

Madame Sagan lived with Dr. Sagan in Palo Alto until her death from cancer on August 25, 2000.

Though I feel I failed her while she lived, I would like to use this opportunity to share the rest of her remarkable history. This is my tribute to her.

Ginetta Sagan was heavily involved with Amnesty International when I lived with her and I heard her mention it a few times. I didn't realize the sheer scale of what she achieved to further the movement in the United States. Amnesty International had a growing reputation in the U.K., at that time, but was still largely unknown in the U.S. Only eighteen chapters of AIUSA had been formed by 1968, all of them in the eastern U.S., totaling fewer than a thousand members. Madame Sagan had been involved in the organization in Washington, D.C. and when she arrived in Atherton she founded the U.S.'s 19th chapter, holding its meetings in her living room.

In 1971 she organized a concert with singer Joan Baez, one of her Atherton neighbors, to raise money for Greek political prisoners. The concert drew more than 10,000 people. In her memoirs, *And a Voice to Sing With*, Joan Baez describes Ginetta Sagan during the period as having 'the gift of an active mind, a love of life and beauty, an unbreakable spirit, and a faith in people very much like that of Anne Frank.'

In the three years that followed, Madame Sagan travelled throughout the American West, founding seventy-five more AI chapters. By 1978, AIUSA's membership had increased to 70,000, more than a hundred times that of a decade before. An AI spokesman later attributed Ginetta Sagan with doing more than anyone to establish Amnesty International in the United States, adding that, 'I think she has probably organized more people than anyone else in the human rights movement globally.' She also founded the organization's first newsletter, *Matchbox*, in 1973.

In later years Madame Sagan became a figure of controversy from the right, and later from the left, in the 1970's when she shifted her focus from protesting abuses by American forces in the Vietnam War to protesting about the abuses of North Vietnamese re-education camps following the war. A colleague remembers fellow anti-war activists being furious that she dared to criticize the new Vietnamese communist regime in the same terms she had criticized the U.S. Armed Forces, and she later remembered accusations that she was a fascist or undercover CIA operative. Over the next decade she also advocated on behalf of prisoners in Chile, the U.S.S.R., Poland, and Greece. She served on the AIUSA National Board of Directors from 1983-87. In 1994, she was elected the organization's Honorary Chair of the Board.

In addition to her work with Amnesty International Madame Sagan founded the Aurora Foundation, which investigates and publicizes incidents of human rights abuses. In 1987 she won a Jefferson Award for Public Service in the category of 'Greatest Public Service Benefiting the Disadvantaged' and in 1996 President Bill Clinton awarded her the Presidential Medal of Freedom, the highest civilian honor in the U.S. In the citation he stated, 'Ginetta Sagan's name is synonymous with the fight for human rights around the world. She represents to all the triumph of the human spirit over tyranny.'

The same year she was awarded the Grand Ufficiale Ordine al Merito della Repubblica Italiana, Italy's highest honor.

A truly remarkable woman. I am so sad we could not have given each other more.

When I left, my hopes were high that I would be moving to a better family. I didn't want to set my expectations too high, to help mitigate any disappointment. Little did I know what pain awaited me. I would have a short glimpse of living in Camelot, only to have those hopes and dreams crushed.

9

And so, I was on my way to another family. I had not visited with either of my parents while I was in the custodial care of Jewish Family Services. I felt let down and completely abandoned by my family. Following the death of my sister I sincerely believed they should have made more of an effort to be with me. Sadly, it wasn't to be.

The new family was named the Normans. They were completely different to Mr. and Mrs. Sagan. Seth and Natalie and their two adopted girls, Margie and Hannah, seemed very open, warm and thoughtful. I thought I was going to get along just fine. When I first arrived, I thought I had found Camelot. Though this was a bit after the time the Kennedys heralded a time of gentile living, the hope of living that myth was still alive. It was the height of the 60's counterculture and everyone guessed that a perfect family was impossible, though it was hard to completely give up the hope of familial happiness.

Seth wasn't particularly pleasant to look at, a small gnome-like man with one or two prominent warts on his face. His skin shade was very dark and his hair greasy with tight curls. His looks were off-putting. It seemed he immediately tried to win me over by telling me I could use his car and assuring me that I would have a great deal of freedom. That did the trick. This was so different from the lock and key environment of the psychiatric hospital and the constant restraints the Sagans placed on me. I really had my hopes up.

Natalie was the quintessential Jewish housewife, a real talker, a little fat, and always showing a generous spirit. Within those first few days I was introduced to Seth's secretary, Barbara. Something weird seemed to be going on there. Barbara would sit on Seth's lap in front of Natalie and, shockingly, it was considered totally acceptable. I thought things were a little too cozy, but I did not want to burst my bubble.

I had finished my high school diploma at night, and I was happy to attend college at Montgomery Jr. College, in Takoma Park, Maryland. While at the Sagans, I attended a vocational course for computer programming that proved to be completely useless in the marketplace. One needed a college degree to get a decent job as a computer programmer; four years of intense study as opposed to nine months in a classroom with a substandard curriculum. It seems that Vocational Rehabilitation, the government agency that paid for my education, was fooled into funding a completely useless program. They wasted my time and their money.

Attending Junior College was a perfect experience for me. I took on the pre-Med program, declaring Biology as my major. I loved it! I could literally spend hours gazing into the microscope, peering at a microscopic world like a giant voyeur, entertained by the quirky movements of these tiny creatures. One of my favorite spectacles was watching the volvoxes, a globe shaped organism, gently tumbling around in their solution. I could hear the New World Symphony play in my head as I watched these creatures perform for me.

In addition to loving my studies, there was another bonanza that awaited me. Student politics. It turned out that I was a natural. I immediately became involved with running to be elected to the student senate. Not only did I run, but I won. I think my biggest advantage was that nobody knew me. I wore a large campaign button that said, 'Vote for Me!'. I put up a number of posters with my name on it. I made a dynamic speech the day before election, and the next thing I knew *I was a senator in the student government.* I was on a winning streak!

For the first time in my memory, I was really happy. And it just seemed to build. One ordinary day, I experienced a mystical moment through the magic of Leonard Cohen's poetry. Let me explain.

I met a guy who was a bit older than me. I can't remember where we were hanging out, but it was close enough to where I grew up that we walked to the edge of the reservoir I knew so well. It would be the first and last time I met him, but now, over fifty years later , I still cherish the magic of that moment. We sat down on a sandy patch, and I offered to share an orange that I brought with me.

'You remind me of Suzanne.'

'Who is she'

'She's the heroine of a song by my hero, Leonard Cohen.'

I confessed my ignorance, and he recited it all to me.

When he told me how 'Suzanne gets you on her wavelength and lets the river answer that you've always been her lover' it was too much for me. In that instant I loved him, Suzanne and Leonard Cohen. It's hard to explain how not being intimate with him on the spot was more powerful than if we had made love. I had already cheapened sex. Wanting him without fucking him was way more powerful. In my convoluted psyche, it elevated him, me and that moment.

My nose was a little runny. Probably unshed tears, but he saw that I was sniffing, and offered me his white cotton handkerchief. Then we parted. Though I never saw him again, I never forgot him. I memorialized that moment by scotch taping his handkerchief into a scrapbook I was keeping. Whenever I heard 'Suzanne', I always recaptured the sanctity of that moment.

In the beginning things were great with the Normans and the new freedom Seth had promised me, materialized. He pretty much let me do anything I wanted to do. At that time, I had started to collect finches, small colorful birds. Seth even allowed me to purchase a large flight cage, in which they lived. I always loved having pets and though I had hoped to become a veterinarian, I changed my focus to becoming a physician. It gave me something to aim for, something to study towards.

The Normans also welcomed my friends into the house too and what's more, treated them like adults, and encouraged us to mix with their friends, especially Seth's secretary, Barbara.

One day my best friend Pammy, from Hawthorne, and I decided to take up Barbara's invitation to visit her at her apartment. Barbara was in her late twenties or early thirties, with curly brown shoulder length hair and a body that was very shapely.

I loved her apartment, even though her taste was absolutely white bread. What stood out most in her decorating scheme was that everything matched. The color scheme was pretty trailer park but nevertheless it was still cool, in a trashy way. There was a wooded landscape painting on the wall that took center stage in the middle of the living room. When I spotted it, I immediately grabbed Pammy's sleeve and whispered to her, 'Take a look at that.' It was the ultimate bad taste in art. In the middle of the fake painting was a real clock. Andy Warhol probably would have loved it because it was so tasteless

We enjoyed our few hours at Barbara's place. We sat around talking and playing cards. Barbara invited us to sleep over. She said she had cleared it with Seth. She pointed out that she had everything we would need to stay overnight, including our own toothbrushes. She showed us a large collection of toothbrushes that were individually wrapped in plastic. She explained that when she brought a guy home she would give him a fresh toothbrush in the morning. A classy touch, she thought.

She was quite boastful about her ability to pick up guys and her extraordinary sex life. What a whore, I thought, but then again this was the 60's! Free love was the way, but even that had its limits. We spent an uneventful night at Barbara's and I suppose I felt quite grown up to be in the company of such a free and liberated older woman. I couldn't help but be troubled about her being so free with Seth. Sitting on Seth's lap seem to be a giveaway that they were sexually involved, but I did not want to believe that. If she was completely free with her affections with strangers she picked up in bars then surely Seth was getting a piece of the action too? I just put it all out of my head. Things were going so well that I did not want anything to break the spell.

(Many years later during a conversation with Pammy, I was told that Barbara had openly admitted that she and Seth regularly slept with each other. She had never said anything to me at the time because she was afraid it would hurt me.)

After I was living with the Normans for months, I witnessed an incident involving their older adopted daughter, Hannah, that greatly disturbed me. I had been out with Mrs. Norman and Margie, the younger adopted daughter. We had been shopping and arrived back at home earlier than expected. When we walked into the living room Hannah was wearing a bikini. This was not a crime in itself, but this was the middle of winter.

Natalie was upset and screamed at her, demanding an explanation. At this point Margie ran from the room. Seth was sitting on the sofa. He was just sitting, no newspaper, the television wasn't switched on. Hannah looked at him as if she wanted him to intervene. I'll never forget the look on Seth's face. Guilt. Natalie never even looked at him, her anger was directed solely at the girl. Whatever they had been doing I'm convinced Seth was behind it. Hannah was tall and skinny with shoulder length straight black hair and I suppose she could be considered sexy in spite of her young age, fifteen years. Her younger sister Margie was honey blonde, twelve years of age and a little heavier, but not fat by any stretch. Both girls were extremely quiet and difficult to interact with.

Nothing really came out of that scene, but it left me wondering about what could have been happening with this young girl. Again, I did not want to blow the illusion of Camelot, so I pushed all of it out of my mind.

Life seemed to go along without incident, until everything came to a cataclysmic ending.

Seth drove me to Montgomery College every day. I was grateful for the ride. I was not very good about waking up in the morning, so he took it on himself to make sure I was awake in time to get dressed and go without making him or I late. Often, he would just rap at my door. That was usually enough to get me in gear. One morning I was moving slowly. I did not jump up when he knocked. The next thing I knew Seth had entered my room and sat down next to me on my bed. I was groggy and not fully awake, so I was slow to comprehend what was going on.

Seth started to rub my back over my covers. Again, I was so sleepy, the inappropriateness of this situation had not hit me. Then he started rubbing my arm, telling me to wake up quietly.

'Don't make any noise,' he said as he edged a little closer. 'Come on Jan, it's time to get up.' He pulled the covers back quickly. I was wearing a t-shirt but was naked underneath. I was still half asleep and groggy and didn't realize that my bare butt was exposed, Seth's eyes took in everything. I remember the look on his face as he gasped.

'You're not wearing any underpants.'

I'm not quite sure what Seth's plans were when he came into my room but I sure as hell knew what he was planning now.

I was fully awake in an instance.

'Get out of my bed!' I screamed as I jumped up and motioned him to get the hell out of my bedroom. He tried to shush me up but gave up and left. We didn't speak until I was fully dressed and in his car on the way to school.

All I said during the ride was one emphatic statement. 'You have plenty of places to sleep in this house. My bed is not one of them!' I left it at that.

I should have known Camelot would not last. I thought I had finally found a happy home but it was not to be.

Within twenty-four hours, Natalie marched me into the kitchen and sat me at the table. I wasn't sure what was coming next, but I knew nothing good was about to happen. I could not have guessed how Seth had twisted the events. 'How dare you accuse Seth of acting inappropriate?'

I could not believe what was happening. To this day, I do not remember any of what was said, but the substance was that I was guilty of making Seth look like a pervert. Somehow, I was accused of accusing him when I said nothing to anyone. Not a word. It didn't take long for me to figure out what had transpired. Seth assumed that I would accuse him of wrongdoing. I guess his best defense was a good offense. He had the upper hand in this and he could manipulate Natalie into believing anything he wanted. Now he wanted to be sure he was held above suspicion. He wanted to maintain the illusion that he could be trusted with other women. And girls. One can only guess what may have happened to the girls.

As it is, Seth did not get away with his bad behavior forever. It turned out that my father's business partner, Roselyn, and my social worker, Coy, went to the same hairdresser. At least ten years after I left the Normans, I told Roselyn the whole story about Seth. Unbeknownst to me, she told Coy about his poor conduct. I was told he was kicked out of the foster program. No idea what happened with Hannah and Margie.

So, there I was, kicked out, with little money and no place to go. I grabbed a copy of the classified section of the *Washington Post* and started to look for rooms for rent. I saw an ad for a room in a commune in Washington D.C. It was owned by Kent State College and primarily meant for use by students, but after I explained my situation, they said they would be glad to meet with me.

I had very little money, but somehow I got to the house. It was in an iffy neighborhood in northwest Washington D.C. Not really bad during the day, but at night it seemed to be loaded with junkies and bootleggers. It honestly didn't matter. I need a refuge.

This was the very first room that I could truly call my own. Even though it was in a rough section of Washington D.C., I loved it. It was furnished too, so it did not matter that I only owned a little bit of clothing. I had no money to rent the room but they trusted me for the rent so I was okay. I had a nice feeling about my new place. My life was coming together. Next item of business was employment, so I went looking for work the following morning and immediately found a job as a cocktail waitress. I was offered the job at the interview and was ecstatic! I couldn't wait to get back to the commune to tell everyone.

I wanted to make my new room my own, so I painted one wall black and put up posters. I did have a small record player, and a few albums. My favorite albums were *In-A-Gadda-Da-Vida* by the Iron Butterfly, *Mellow Yellow* by Donovan and *Their Satanic Majesties Request* by the Rolling Stones. I lay on my bed for hours listening to the lyrics and nobody minded how often I played the same tunes or how loud it was.

Even though I began my music education with folk and the classics, the music from the 60's appealed to me in a way that went beyond what the classics could do for me. I had not yet discovered jazz. Rock 'n' roll was special. It was angry and out of control, and it moved me. Music has always been important in my life. It always felt like a primal way for me to emote my feelings. The classics seemed to soothe me. Rock 'n' roll helped me release my demons.

Music shaped my life in many ways. Looking back at my piano teacher, Gertrude, I was able to see that she taught me more than just music. She gave me life lessons. She really helped me to work on my self-esteem, reminding me to pay attention to what was important in life. I had to keep my nails short to play, which bothered me, because long nails were the fashion. Gertrude put it all in perspective. My long nails may look pretty, but the clicking noise they made ruined my playing. The bigger life lesson was how trivial vanity was, and is. She helped me put my life into perspective with small examples like that. I really integrated her message about values. She helped shape my character as much as she developed my musicianship.

A cute story I remember was how Gertrude joked about her son's name. Her last name was Bloch, pronounced Block. She said she regretted not naming him Johann Sebastian Bloch. I'm sure that was tongue in cheek.

Getting back to my first home of my own; I don't remember much about the other occupants at the commune. Mostly they were students from Ohio who had attended Kent State and were visiting Washington D.C. Everyone seemed to have their own lives and didn't have much to do with me. That was, everybody except this one amazing man, who I will call Kent. He was very special to me.

He was tall and shy, with silky dark hair, quiet and extremely sexy. Kent was very open and candid, qualities I really appreciated. He was an artist and was happy to share his amazing drawings with me. A lot of them were cartoonish representations of the forces of nature. Eros and Pathos were also common themes. Eros was portrayed as figure riding a large penis. That image stayed with me for some time. Kent's message was sacred to him, and I felt special that he shared his heart with me.

After my previous experiences with acid, I wasn't expecting much from it and yet I still heard people talking about how 'far out' their acid trips were. It kept me curious.

I was at the Kent State commune when a guy offered me a hit of blotter acid. I met him at the commune, where he was hanging with a friend, Julian, who lived in the commune. I was a bit reluctant to try the acid at first but after a little gentle persuasion from the two of the, I took it. I didn't expect too much. Within an hour something strange started to happen. I started feeling speeded up and giddy. Everything seemed amazing as we slumped onto a large sofa and began laughing. I looked around and all the colors seemed heightened, more intense. The guy and his buddy radiated energy and colors. Something strange was happening. They seemed to know exactly what I was going through. I was conscious of them staring at me, laughing at my reaction to what was to be my first real trip.

They started to undress.

'What are you doing?' I asked.

'We're taking a shower.'

'Together?'

'Yes, the three of us.'

He explained that what I was feeling at that moment would be heightened by the sensation of water on my naked body. I couldn't wait to tear my clothes off as we all headed towards the shower, throwing our clothes off en route. It was amazing to feel the water beating on my skin and my face, it was so exhilarating, making my whole body tingle with pleasure. In fact, the guys had to regularly pull my head out of the water spray because I kept enjoying it so much I forgot about the part where I needed to breathe. We were in there for what seemed like hours. I later heard that we flooded the basement below us with our ridiculously long shower. I don't know what happened to the other guy but after a while I was alone with Julian and I decided to go to my bedroom. I'm glad that we did. For whatever reason I started coming down. I suddenly became terribly afraid and I thought something terrible was going to happen. He figured out exactly how to cure me from crashing. He'd been there before he assured me, and was an expert.

I was frightened. 'Help me please.'

He climbed on top of me and I felt his stiff penis pressing into my stomach.

'We need to make love,' he said. 'Over and over again, it's the only cure.'

And he was right! As long as we were making love, I felt fine. He seemed to have an insatiable appetite and we made love for hours.

The sequence of events was repeated over and over again. I would start to freak out and he would push me onto my back and climb on top of me. And it worked. The lovemaking would distract me and take my mind off the awful things that were flying around my head and I'd start to feel better. When we stopped, my brain drifted back towards the dark side. It was exhausting work but I begged him for more. At one point I went out of the room and when I came back I looked at his thin body lying on the bed under the covers and I thought he was dead. I thought I had fucked him to death!

It was getting late in the day and he couldn't take any more. He wanted to leave and begged me to let him go, so I did. After he left, I put on my baby doll pink nightie, nothing else, and stood out on my bedroom's balcony so that I could watch people go by in the street. Everybody looked fascinating, their clothes and hair big and vibrant, shimmering seductively as the last rays of the sun glistened on them. The sun touched every single person and I stood grinning at them for far too long. The reality was that these were drug dealers and bootleggers, dangerous people who wouldn't think twice of taking advantage of a spaced-out teenager in an over-short pink nightie. I dread to think what I looked like. I knew there were terrible people down there but to me they all looked amazing.

The acid had worked and at last I could relate to the other stories I'd heard from my friends and peers. It wasn't so much that there were things there that I couldn't see otherwise, my trip was just a heightened sensory experience and everything looked super beautiful, vivid, sharper, and more colorful than anything I'd ever seen before. The shower experience was still so fresh in my mind. It was all amazing. I finally fell asleep and woke up the next day feeling wasted, so I just stayed in bed for the next twenty-four hours.

A painful event in American history took place while we were living at the commune. Dr. Martin Luther King Jr. was assassinated. I was a longtime admirer of Dr. King. I cried when I first heard his 'I Have a Dream' speech. I know he saw his death coming. In his last ever speech, when he described how he went to the mountain top, I knew G!d talked to him. He knew he was going to G!d. It was as if he was shown his assassination and was prepared to meet his maker. He knew his time was short, and Dr. King shared that he was not afraid. He was not afraid for himself, though he should have been afraid for the people he left behind. If Dr. King could see what happened to this country since we lost his moral leadership, he would have been very afraid for the future of America. Since his death, modern technology has given a megaphone to political bullies. Terrible people like Alex Jones and Donald Trump preach hate and foment chaos. The way politics are played today would have sickened Dr. King, no doubt.

Dr. King was monumental in the civil rights movement, though I was disappointed that he hadn't become involved in the anti-war protest. I understand it was more important for him to stay focused on black equality and civil rights, but I felt let down because I know he supported our position on peace. He only made one Vietnam speech that I know of, exactly one year before his death, and that felt like a token effort.

I was with Pammy at her house when we heard that Dr. King was dead. Riots began immediately. We heard about the tanks rolling onto the streets of D.C. and that martial law had been declared, though we honestly had no idea what that meant. It was so sad because it seems that the black people were burning down their own neighborhoods. We wondered why they didn't burn down posh white neighborhoods like

Chevy Chase or Georgetown. I was afraid to go to Washington until weeks after everything quieted down.

I felt ill. I couldn't wrap my head around the thought that I would never hear or see this great American hero again. I couldn't handle losing another hero. The death of Kennedy had been a huge blow to my faith in the American Dream. President John F. Kennedy was assassinated when I was thirteen, approximately one and a half years after my sister died. My sister's death heralded the dissolution of my family. Kennedy's death seemed to be the end of hope for an elegant social order, where our country was presided over by the grace of an aristocratic first family. Dr. King's death seemed to announce the end of hope for a moral America. In Vietnam we saw the might of the CIA. Those of us who were politically in the know recognized their use of assassination as a political tool. Air America, owned and operated by the CIA, was apparently responsible for trafficking heroin, with the proceeds going who knows where. The Central Intelligence Agency was trying to seize control of the infamous 'Golden Triangle,' an area of around 367,000 square miles that overlapped the mountains of three countries of southeast Asia, and the most extensive opium-producing area of the world since the fifties. Most of the world's heroin came from the Golden Triangle. The CIA together with various elements of organized crime were shipping huge amounts of heroin out of that area and into America.

The Vietnam War was run by lies. I didn't understand why it was necessary to try to deceive the public about the military's actions, because we knew about the covert operations that bombed Laos and Cambodia despite the assurances to the contrary.

I honestly don't remember the sources for what passed as 'common knowledge' back then. I was a vociferous reader, and certainly the underground press, *Washington Post* and information from my friends would have fueled most of what I knew. Maybe even listening to Mort Saul could have furnished me with a great deal of truth. Remember, this was before the internet was born. Before we had a myriad of information at our fingertips. I honestly don't know how we found the truth, but we did.

10

At the beginning of my time on Montgomery College's campus, I did not connect with people who cared about the war in Vietnam. It would take important events that transpired with the war, to get more and more students caring about the need to end this immoral war.

It was 1969 when details emerged about one of the most horrific atrocities of the Vietnam War, namely the My Lai Massacre. A company of American soldiers brutally killed the majority of the population of the South Vietnamese hamlet of My Lai. The incident took place a year before anyone heard about it. The massacre was a shameful war crime, but the cover-up that ensued catapulted it all into a crime against humanity that rivaled Nazi war crimes. As many as five-hundred people, including women, children and the elderly, were killed in what was now being called the My Lai Massacre. It was becoming clear that the Pentagon and high-ranking U.S. Army officers had covered up the events of that day until a soldier who could no longer keep quiet came forward with details of this senseless, brutal massacre of defenseless civilians. His revelations sparked a wave of international outrage and led to a special investigation into the matter. In 1970, a U.S. Army Board charged fourteen officers with crimes related to the events at My Lai. The outcome would only produce one conviction. The brutality of the My Lai killings and the extent of the cover-up increased growing anti-war sentiment at home in the United States. Most of the outrage was expressed at colleges and universities through marches and organized protests. As more and more details came out we were sickened that U.S. soldiers, and in particular their commanders, could have acted in this way. The outcry against the war increased and was not limited to the intellectuals. It seemed the tide of public opinion was turning against this war.

I was focused on events in Vietnam, but the wider scope of politics was also grabbing my attention. I was particularly captivated by an early leader of the Black Panther Party. He was also the author of *Soul on Ice*, my hero, Eldridge Cleaver. While I only read bits and pieces of his book, which was written while he was at Folsom Prison, I was always quick to quote the axiom of my existence which I borrowed from his work, 'You either have to be part of the solution, or you're going to be part of the problem'. This sentiment has guided me since I first heard it back in the 60's. I believed in my heart of hearts that not contributing to the solution of a problem was as bad as creating the problem.

Activism was my credo. There was never a good excuse to be passive. I believed then, as I do now, that inaction is at the heart of so much that is wrong in society. People seem to feel no responsibility for others. At the heart of my belief system is that we are all brothers and sisters, that is, part of the Family of Man.

I stayed busy with politics, mostly gathering information. Fortunately, I did not let anything interfere with my schoolwork. Despite my drug abuse I did surprisingly well and made honors and the Dean's list. Academically things were going very well. I enjoyed my time in school, and managed to have some special extracurricular activity.

One of my most exciting misadventures transpired with the lab assistant who was in charge of all the lab and science facilities. Larry was extremely cool. We had no illusions about our relationship, as he was married. Our relationship was strictly physical, which was fine. He held the keys to the school planetarium, which became our favorite place to have sex. In it he would create a light show using an electrical storm that his equipment made come to life. That would become an exciting backdrop for some truly wicked sex. Every place in the planetarium was game for fucking. Mostly we would use the seats, though the floor worked out well too. Fortunately, we never got caught. In time we got tired of it, and it was on to the next.

The weekends were still an open invitation to the drug scene. Stoned or not, I was always extremely concerned about Vietnam and all the political implications of our government supporting what I considered an unjust and illegal war. I sincerely believed that the Vietnam War was a civil war and we had no business being in the middle of it. I knew we were there for our own gain. Our involvement had nothing to do with helping the Vietnamese people. It was sold to the American people as a fight against the bogeymen, the communists. I knew that we had no business going in there, sacrificing young American lives and slaughtering innocent women and children. The domino theory, which predicted a sequential fall to communism with all the governments in the countries surrounding Vietnam, was a myth. That theory was used to justify the escalation of the war. It was a lie! We needed to get out.

It was then that I learned the most important fact of political life. If the government can sell fear to the public, they can sell you anything. Simple. Fear was the government's most important war propaganda. Frighten the masses and they will do your bidding. I felt it was my job to fight fear with truth. We needed to take our voices to the streets and let the American people see that the government was creating a false narrative to suit their own purposes. Sell them fear and you can sell them *anything*! Please remember their motto.

On May 1, a huge demonstration was organized at Kent State University in Ohio. Mostly it came off peacefully, however during the evening the students mingled with a biker gang in the center of town. Fueled by drugs and alcohol, violence escalated and bricks and bottles were thrown at the police. The next day, Kent's mayor declared a state of emergency, asking the governor to send in the national guard to secure law and order. This was seen as a provocative move by the students, who decided to stage further protests the next day. On May 3, Governor James Rhodes held a press conference vilifying the student protestors and threatening a state of emergency, which would in effect ban all types of demonstrations. He called the protestors un-Americans who were trying to destroy higher education in Ohio. He continued, 'They were the worst type of people we harbor in America, worse than the brownshirts and the communists.'

That night the national guard ordered a curfew and dispersed the protestors with tear gas. The following day the protestors were back. We watched the press conferences on television as a series of suited individuals condemned the protests.

On May 4, the war came to the streets of America as the national guard fired a total of sixty-seven shots into the protestors. Four students were murdered: William Schroeder, Sandra Sheuer, Allison Krause and Jeffrey Miller. Another thirteen were wounded. The unthinkable had happened: American soldiers had turned their guns on American students. We were all in shock. Who kills a student? This action could not be tolerated. I was at Montgomery College when I heard about the murders. I knew we had to do something. I was talking with a few of my friends in class and I begged them to follow me. We stopped the lesson in session, left that class and proceeded to walk into another classroom that was in session. The teacher ordered me from the room but I ignored him.

I spoke, 'Fellow students, please follow me. We cannot allow things to go on as they are. We are calling for a student strike.'

I went from classroom to classroom. The teachers ordered me out and I ignored them all, begging people to follow me. We gathered up a crowd of about forty to fifty people at that point as not all the students rallied to my call. Some were frightened, they didn't want more protests and demonstrations, violence and more shootings. We went to the cafeteria to plot our strategy and afterwards went to administration and demanded a room to operate from. We decided our most important function would be to publish and to disseminate information that would help coordinate protests and demonstrations. Over the next few weeks my politics became my world.

We formed a group that went to all the surrounding colleges to meet with other students who were trying to seize this opportunity to create a force for good. We honestly had no big picture plan. We saw ourselves as little and fringe because we attended a small community junior college. We were determined to do our best. Me and my comrades fanned out to the different colleges to meet with like-minded students to see how we could make the most of this student strike. We wanted America to do better and we knew we had to be the change we wanted to see.

All kinds of different political factions literally came out of the woodwork. I could not believe the different political forces that were already at work in America. There were Black Panthers and White Panthers, there were communists, people who followed Che Guevara, people who followed Mao. Almost any political faction one could imagine emerged, and peace was not necessarily their goal. They mostly seemed to follow their own political doctrine, joining with the students to try and co-opt us for their own political purposes. At first I assumed that because they emerged during our efforts, which were clearly motivated by peace, that they would also have peace as their highest priority. *Wrong!* For many it wasn't so much a pro-peace movement. It was just being anti-American.

It became clear that information gathering and publishing was important, so we set up our little room as a headquarters for information. We created a newsletter that disseminated information to the other schools. Looking back, it is hard for me to be specific about the details of what we did. This was before the internet, so whatever we produced was hard copy, duplicated on paper and physically handed out. I do remember one amusing scene where the vice principal entered our room to check in on what we were up to. I pointed to a stack of papers and told him these were the newsletters we produced. He offered to buy one and handed me a quarter.

'Just see this money doesn't go to a Black Panther or someone else who might kill me.' He let out a weak chuckle.

I assured him he was safe. Actually, the money
went for our wine.

One of the most interesting presentations that took place came from Nader's Raiders. Ralph Nader had been working extremely hard at uncovering the corruption in government. He unearthed the cover-up in the auto industry over the unsafe Chevrolet Corvair in his book, *Unsafe at any Speed*. The effort to come to our campus was just one of many of his campaigns. Young college students came and talked to us on his behalf. Their message was basically for us to get dressed up and look exactly like the straight people so we could work on change from the inside of government, kind of like termites. We were all excited because we believed that great changes were in the air. We wanted to make a difference. We wanted to weed out corruption, like Nader's Raiders. We wanted to turn America around.

The deaths of the four American students in Ohio really shook the nation's young people. I heard a story about how

Neil Young took a walk in his local woods and proceeded to compose a song with the incredibly haunting chorus line, *Four dead in Ohio*. It was performed by Crosby, Stills, Nash, and Young, and became the protest anthem of our generation. It was said that David Crosby cried when the group finished the recording session.

Those lyrics are still embedded in my heart.

I paid a dear price for my part in the student strike. As mentioned, I had received honors and made the dean's list because of my exemplary grades. My best friend Pam attended George Washington University, and they were not academically penalized for participating in the strike. However, I received straight zeros for that semester, destroying any hope that my pre-Med curriculum would be a ticket to medical school. I felt beyond disappointed. I felt destroyed, because all my efforts to make changes failed, and my future looked bleak.

The war dragged on. More deaths, more body bags arriving on American soil, more horrific pictures of war. The most memorable was a Vietnamese child on fire from napalm, running naked in the street.

I couldn't take much more; the entire world seemed to be turning a blind eye.

11

I threw myself into the peace cause. Even though it wasn't clear that the demonstrations were effective, as a follower of Gandhi's belief in non-violence, I saw no other path. I had heard about the teachings of Gandhi, though I was more familiar with Dr. Martin Luther King Jr. I would later learn that Dr. King's philosophy of non-violence was directly shaped by the teachings of Gandhi, so it behooved me to investigate his writing. There were many mystical influences that helped shape my activism, including Yogananda's *Autobiography of a Yogi* and the many books of Carlos Castañeda, a mystical shaman and healer. The more I reinforced my belief in universal mystical healing powers, the more I believed that divine forces would guide my actions as long as my heart was pure and my hands were free from violence.

While it is true that the teachings of the mystics were a bedrock for my beliefs, in April of 1971, the Yippie founder Abbie Hoffman's *Steal This Book* would have a huge impact on my next participation in a protest. Abbie gave me a new perspective on civil disobedience. He promoted humor as a political strategy. His way to fight back included a comedic twist. If it was funny and it made you laugh, then the sting was taken out of fighting back.

He thought you should make a statement that cost the opposition money. Doing it with levity made it okay. For instance, one way to lodge a protest against corporate America was to use the prepaid postcards that you found in magazines. They were meant to be mailed in with your personal information and a request to be contacted in response to an ad. Instead he suggested you glue the postcard to a brick, mail it in and stick the company with the cost of postage. If enough bricks were mailed you could bankrupt the business.

Then there was the plot to destroy banks. Abbie said that it was illegal for anyone to open a deposit box, other than the key holder. So, you rent a deposit box for a few years, and then put a dead fish in the box. Supposedly the bank could not legally remove the contents of the box, and when the smell was bad enough, the bank's only option was to move.

This mischievous method of conveying our disdain appealed to a great many of us hippies. We were angry and wanted to fight back.

We were coming up to the anniversary of the Kent State and Jackson State massacres. The anger and hurt needed expression. This time we were going to have a more militant demonstration. It was May Day 1971 and May Day was about disruption. We headed for Washington D.C. with a focus on Georgetown, a posh section of Washington. We were going to do whatever we could to stop the government, stop the people, stop everything, and get attention. I hooked up with a friend, John, and we headed to Georgetown to join in the fray. We knew it was going to be dangerous but we didn't care. We heard the government had been given a heads-up so they put into effect a plan that had been developed to combat urban disorders. There were literally thousands of police and troops everywhere you looked.

One sight that will be forever carved into my memory was a cop on a scooter driving into groups of people on foot, mowing them down painfully. Now and then you could hear a cop shouting, 'National Guard 4 - Hippies nothing!' This was a reference to the four murdered students at Kent State.

John and I stayed close as we walked up the street. Suddenly, out of nowhere, a uniformed D.C. cop ran over to John, pulled out a wooden baton and whacked him on the leg. I couldn't believe what I witnessed. John did absolutely nothing to provoke the attack. Later, when I had a chance to look at his thigh where he had taken the blow, I saw the deep purple of a painful bruise. That bastard was aiming to cripple John.

We wanted to stop the people of Washington from going about their normal lives to get their attention. We came upon a D.C. transit bus that was stopped in traffic. I watched as a tall skinny guy with long wavy hair lifted the back panel and proceeded to rip out the wiring, doing whatever he could to disable it. Everybody around watched and cheered him on and eventually the electrics on the bus gave up and the engine stopped. The poor bus driver had no idea as to what to do as he tried to restart the engine without success. He was stuck in traffic and the cars, vans and trucks behind him were going nowhere either. They vented their anger and frustration, shaking fists out of windows and blaring their horns. Finally, after about five minutes the driver threw his hands up in disgust, got out of the bus and started to walk away. Everybody cheered and clapped him on his way as he cursed and swore at anyone and everyone.

Mostly we spent the day dodging cops' batons and trying to stop the traffic, to bring Washington to gridlock. Out of the corner of my eye I saw a cop lob what looked like a small bowling ball which headed straight for me. It didn't dawn on me that he wasn't bowling, so I just kept walking towards it. Suddenly it exploded into a thick cloud. I still didn't register what it was so I kept walking towards it until I walked into the cloud at its densest point. I realized too late that it was teargas when I felt as if a thousand needles had been pushed into my eyeballs. The pain was searing, I collapsed and fell to my knees, crying out and rubbing my eye sockets, which was the worst thing I could have done. Panic erupted around me, I heard police charging and skulls being cracked with batons and felt sure that my turn was fast approaching. Fortunately for me there were medics present and I felt two sets of hands lift me up from the ground and drag me away. When I opened my eyes, I saw a young man in a white lab coat. He had bottles of water and started pouring them over my face to try to reduce the pain. It burned like hell and took me easily half an hour before I felt like a human being again.

The TV cameras were there, as was the international press, and we were determined to give them something to report.

We hung in until dark. We had two more violent encounters with the police, but this time we fared a little better and suffered only some glancing blows from a few boots and fists. We were exhausted, in pain and completely done in. My eyes still smarted. I told John I needed to get home, go to bed, and close my eyes for a week. Reluctantly he agreed. The streets were strewn with the debris from the day and looked so different from the streets we'd walked earlier in the day. We searched for John's car and miraculously found it in one piece. We drove to his apartment. Despite the pain and exhaustion, we managed to muster just enough energy to make love and then fell asleep. It had been a good day all round.

I want to be clear that my anger was not directed towards the soldiers. I didn't dislike the U.S. troops, but was angry with the government that used them. As I've said in the past, I felt that most of the soldiers, nearly all working class, were as much victims as the Vietnamese people they were killing.

In this time, I lived in a big house in Takoma Park with two former Marines I met in school. They were a little over twenty years old and never ever talked about their experiences in Vietnam, except once. They had come back from Vietnam with an injury each. Both had burns going from the tips of their fingers to the top of their forearms. Hudson was burned on his right and Joe was burnt on the left. When I say burned, I mean fried to a crisp. Both wore custom-made black leather gloves that covered and protected every inch of burned flesh. I thought it was strange to have identical gloves on opposite arms and one night over a few joints I finally asked them what had happened. Hudson blew a long plume of smoke high into the air and explained.

They were working together on a rocket launcher. Hudson was passing a shell to Joe to load it when they took enemy fire. They were both blown into unconsciousness, and were never totally clear about what happened, but when they awoke in hospital, they found they had almost identical injuries but on opposite sides. It created an incredible bond, and they vowed to stay together after they returned

They were both laughing about the incident that had maimed them. They seemed to be coping well. There were many maimed soldiers who did not fare as well, and struggled for many years with depression and PTSD.

One day they announced that an ambulance would be bringing an old Vietnam war comrade to the house.

'An ambulance?' I enquired. 'He must be pretty bad?'

'He's well fucked up,' Joe said. 'Stepped on a land mine.'

When the ambulance arrived and they unloaded their buddy I could see exactly what they meant. Poor Irwin was in a full plaster cast, lying on a stretcher. He'd broken both legs, numerous ribs, both arms, several vertebrae and sustained a fracture to his skull. The only piece of his body that hadn't sustained serious injury was his groin and the hospital had left a big hole in the plaster so he was able to take a leak. They lifted him onto a bed they had moved into the living room and I took a chair and sat down beside him. Almost as soon as I started talking to him he started shaking.

His buddies were laughing at him as he explained he had been in Vietnam for three months and in a military field hospital for over six months and I was the first woman he'd gotten close to in a long time.

I was curious. This boy was twenty years old and this was the 60's, a time of sexual revolution. 'Anything goes,' I thought.

'So you haven't been around girls for how long?'

'Over eight months.'

I stood up.

'Joe, Hudson, you're gonna have to leave the room.'

'Why?'

'Because I want to get to know your friend.'

They politely left and we were alone. Irwin continued to shake until I finally convinced him to relax. We talked and talked about everything and nothing. I had read the book, *Candy*, wherein the protagonist believed in the healing powers of a mercy fuck. At one point she even screwed a repulsive dwarf out of kindness. All in the pursuit of the healing powers of love.

Obviously, Irwin could use some of this magic.

It was clear. He'd forgotten he was a man. I'm sure the major damage to his body undermined the notion that he was manly or had sex appeal. I would fix that. Without a lot of talk, I removed the blanket to reveal a very quiet crotch.

I could see I was going to have to do all the work.

I knew it wouldn't take much work to magically turn a flaccid penis into an upstanding member of the Marines, at attention!

I realized I had to be quite gentle with him. I removed his loose-fitting pajamas. There was quite a large hole in the plaster cast. Poking through without any more coaxing from me was a large, stiff penis. I removed my underpants and climbed up onto the bed, straddling him and guided him into me. He lay there in ecstasy, as still as a corpse while I brought him to orgasm. It took no more than five minutes. The poor man. When we were finished I pulled on my panties, buttoned him up and called Joe and Hudson back into the room. It was all a big joke to them but I was pleased to have helped Irwin on the road to recovery.

A week later, when he was returned to Walter Reed Hospital, I went to visit Irwin. He couldn't wait to propose to me. I knew I had to set him straight without hurting his feelings. I explained that though I was sexually attracted to him, we were much too different to contemplate marriage. I left after wishing him the best. Later I found out he fell in love with one of his nurses and they married. I would like to believe I did my part in restoring his sense of worth.

A few weeks after the Georgetown demonstration, I met who I thought was the first real love of my life, a man named Benim. When we met Ben was attending Montgomery College and driving a cab to make money. I had no real idea about his background, other than what he told me. He said that his father was a good friend of the shah of Iran. When the shah was deposed, his family and other families had to flee for their lives. Many of them came to America. I remember one friend of his, a dark, hulking and brooding guy who never smiled. Ben said that his father had been one of the top generals in the secret Persian army. This guy was so scary looking. I really did not understand anything about Iranian politics at the time but it did seem to me that these were people who came from money and power, and had suddenly found themselves having to start their lives over in America. Though it was clearly below his station, that was why Ben had to drive taxis. I knew nothing about the corruption and torture that took place under the shah. If I had, it might have given me an insight into Ben's true personality. At the time I was completely blinded by love. He just seemed like somebody who really liked me. He paid constant attention to me and never stopped complimenting me. He made love to me for hours. That was enough for me, I simply adored him. He was everything I wanted in a man and I was completely in love.

I saw him on and off for about two years. He seemed to disappear quite often, said he had to return to Iran, or to meet with his father in another part of the country. I never really understood his absences, but I was so happy to be with him that I never asked any questions and accepted it. I was young and in love, the happiest I'd ever been.

He took me to a nice apartment in Silver Spring, Maryland over the course of a few months. It was large and very beautifully furnished and I loved it. It was mainly a place we would go to for lovemaking. He'd cook me dinner and fuss over me and afterwards we'd always go to bed. On the odd occasion I would see his roommate but we mostly had the place to ourselves.

I'm not sure what aroused my suspicion, but one night I went to his apartment to find him so that I could spend time with him. I usually just waited for him to contact me but there had been a long stretch since we had spent any time together and I was beginning to wonder if something was up.

I knocked at the door and his roommate answered.

'Ben is not at home,' he said, 'but you can come in if you like.'

I walked in and looked around to see if I could see any telltale signs that Ben had been there. There was nothing, no coat, shoes, nothing.

'Where in the heck is Ben?' I queried.

'At the library.'

'The library is closed. It's after 6 o'clock.' I was starting to get mad.

'Then he's probably at somebody's house, studying.'

'I don't believe you.'

I looked around the apartment again, surely there was something that would give me a clue. Just then I spied Ben's address book on the coffee table and made a grab for it. When I opened it, I saw that it was all in Farsi. 'If you don't call Ben right now, I'm going to call every single phone number in this book until I get him!'

His roommate was shaking his head, telling me not to get upset.

I looked at the book again. Of course, the numbers alongside the names weren't in Farsi. I recognized one that I thought I had called in the past. Sure enough, alongside was a short word. It had to be Ben. 'That's his number, isn't it?'

More shaking of the head.

'Right, give me the phone. I'm calling him right now.'

'Don't do that. Let me call him, let me talk to him first,' he said as he picked up the phone.

He punched in the number and started talking to someone in Farsi. The next thing I knew he handed me the phone. 'It's Ben.'

I was trembling as I took the phone and something told me that my beautiful world was about to come crashing down around me. 'Ben, what the hell is going on and why aren't you here at your house?'

'I am home,' he said in a quiet voice.

'But...I don't understand. This is your house, this is where we meet, this is where we -'

'Wait until I see you. I'll explain.'

He didn't need to explain. I slammed down the phone. Everything was clear. I turned to his friend.

'He's married, right?!' I screamed.

The silence from his friend told me everything I needed to know.

I ran out of the apartment in a flood of tears. This was my worst nightmare. The years of trust, those magical moments, the tender lovemaking meant nothing to him as all the while he had a wife waiting for him back home.

I wished I were dead

12

At the time I found out about Ben I was back living with my father.

I made it to my car, but just slumped behind the wheel, crying uncontrollably. It was some time before I was able to compose myself enough to drive. I didn't know what to do at this point. I just climbed into the car and started driving, trying to see the road through my intermittent tears. The next thing I knew I was near Dupont Circle in Washington. I pulled over and parked my car, then walked over to the Roy Rogers, which was a fast food restaurant. I didn't get anything to eat, just ordered a coffee and sat there feeling sorry for myself. I could not believe my life could get worse. The irony was that it was about to do just that.

Within just a few minutes, a short, dirty looking black guy came over to my table. 'Hey, yo yo yo.'

Without thinking I looked up at him and asked, 'Do you know where I can buy some smack?'

Smack was the street name for heroin. I had never tried heroin but it seemed like a good way to stop the pain, or to destroy myself. At that moment I didn't care what happened to me.

'Sure, I can get you whatever you need.' He was with another dude who was slightly taller than him. Both were dressed nondescriptly, just T-shirts and jeans. It was the July 4th weekend and Washington was hotter than hell. They slid into the booth across the table from me.

'I don't have a lot of money. I've never really tried it before, so I don't think I'll need much.'

'Hey, don't worry, we'll fix you up. You're in for a treat.'

'So, where to?' I said.

'We've got the stuff over at my place. It's just five minutes from here.'

The shorter guy did all the talking.

'My car is just parked across the street. I can drive us,' I offered.

'Cool.'

We all walked out to my blue Maverick. As we climbed in I remember thinking how much I hated that car and its plaid seat covers. We drove a few blocks and then they instructed me to park. 'Look, we've got to make sure that you're not a cop so we're going to blindfold you and then we will lead you over to where I live. Is that okay?'

That seemed reasonable so I agreed to be blindfolded. The taller dude had a red bandana around his neck. He removed it then tied it around my head, covering my eyes. They got on either side of me and started walking me down the street. At one point I heard some other footsteps and voices and I wondered what people must've thought about two black guys leading a blindfolded young white girl down the street. I guess they thought nothing of it because I heard their footsteps trail off into the distance.

'Careful now, we're coming to some steps.'

I pushed my way forward, feeling for the steps. I hit something.

'Step up. Step up.'

And so it went until we got to the top of the stairs. They opened the door and gently pushed me along. We walked down a long hallway, then I heard them turn a key and we were inside the room. They took the blindfold off and I could see that I was in a really crummy little boarding room. There was nothing in the room except a bed and a chair with a fan on it. It was hot and humid and it smelled.

I wiped the sweat from my face with the back of my hand. 'So where's the dope?'

I just wanted to score and get the hell out of this place as it was now beginning to scare me.

The taller guy grinned.

'Now, I don't think we are none too worried about no dope.'

'Then I want to go.'

They both laughed. Suddenly it dawned on me how stupid I had been. This was not about me getting dope. This was all about them getting off with the young white girl.

'Look. Don't be stupid. My dad is a D.C. cop. Besides, I am pregnant.'

I knew by now that I was in serious shit and I tried to think of anything that would put them off me. I had started crying hysterically. They weren't happy.

'You've got a pretty face; you want to keep it pretty? Then quit whining. You know what we want so the sooner you get naked, the sooner we get what we want and you can go home.'

I looked towards the door and wondered if I could make a break for it.

One of them noticed.

'Don't think about it bitch.'

He stood up and took off his belt.

'I'm getting impatient, take off you blouse this minute, or you'll be eating the buckle of this belt.'

Between the tears and the sobs, I removed my blouse and then my bra. I stood for a while and after more threats removed everything else. One of the men stripped while the other stood guard at the door. He came towards me and started pawing me before throwing me on the bed and getting on top of me.

They took turns raping me. It seemed to last forever. The entire time they were raping me all I could think about was picking up the fan in the corner of the room and smashing their brains out. I knew at that moment that if I had a gun I would've killed them. What a harsh revelation. I had always pictured myself as a humanitarian, a pacifist, incapable of killing another human being. This was a stark insight into my dark side. I never knew I had the capacity to kill. At that moment, if I had a way, there was no doubt I would have murdered them both.

The ordeal lasted hours; at least three, possibly longer. They'd rest and talk and I'd beg them to let me go but then soon after one of them would grin and announce that he was ready again, my legs would be forced apart and it started all over. It was vile, I was a piece of meat, nothing more.

Then I heard some Spanish voices at the door. People were pounding on it, trying to break it down. I heard one of them say something about wanting a piece of the action and I was petrified that this ordeal could go on forever. Miraculously, the black guys managed to get rid of them with threats of violence.

Finally, the taller guy announced that he'd had enough. As he left, I remember feeling a little relieved but it soon became apparent I'd been left alone with a nut.

He seemed to be kind of doped up and crazy. I didn't know if it was the drugs or his own insanity. Surely two men who were prepared to abuse a girl in this manner were not normal. He kept talking about a girl who did him wrong. The next thing I knew he was talking to me like I was that girl. 'Don't you know if you just love me, I'll treat you right,' he slurred.

I knew the only way to get out of there was to play along with the game. 'Sure, I get it.'

'You don't want to be messing around with no drugs anyway. You can just drink some Jack.'

I assumed he was talking about Jack Daniels. This was my chance. 'You're right, you're right. Why don't we go out and get some Jack or something?'

'Okay baby,' he said. 'Let's go.'

I had been wearing a thin brown corduroy jumper with a shiny purple dress shirt underneath and my bra and panties. My underwear was pretty much destroyed and my top was a crumpled mess so I just put the brown jumper on, pulled on my underpants and was ready to go.

'You know I've got to blindfold you?'

'You don't have to worry about that,' I said.

I wanted to be able to see where they had taken me, these guys had to be stopped. How many girls had they abused in this way?

'No, you got to be blindfolded girl.'

I reluctantly agreed. As he led me down the stairs I slipped and scraped my leg from the ankle to the top of my thigh. I felt something trickling down my leg, it could only have been blood. I did my best to ignore it and keep going. Again, I could hear some peoples' voices and footsteps too, they weren't too far away from me. What were they thinking?

When we stopped walking, I took off my blindfold and we were standing on the passenger side of my car. He looked at me for a second. This was my chance.

'I'm just going to put my stuff in the trunk,' I said.

I walked around to the back of the car. He waited for me by the passenger's side. I walked very slowly, deliberately slow, so as to not arouse suspicion. He could have pounced or changed his mind at any moment and I didn't want that. In slow motion, I put my crumpled blouse in the trunk of my car, closed the lid and then walked around to the driver's side. I slid my key in the lock, sat down, turned the ignition, and as he made for the handle, slammed the gas pedal to the floor. I looked in my rear mirror to see him standing dumbfounded. It was a tiny moment of triumph.

I ran the first few stop lights I encountered, driving like a wild woman. I needed to get as far away from that neighborhood, out of Washington D.C. altogether.

I kept driving until I was over the Maryland line and I could feel I was safely out of Washington D.C. I pulled my car over and threw it into park. I put my head on the steering wheel and just cried and shook. It only took about ten minutes for a cop to show up and investigate why a car was pulled over on Georgia Avenue, in downtown Silver Spring.

'Hey you. What's going on here?'

'Leave me alone.'

'Come on. What's the matter? Obviously, something is wrong.'

'I said leave me alone.' I was getting really mad.

'I am not leaving until I find out what is go on.'

'Leave me alone'

'I'm going nowhere until you tell me why you're in a state.'

I looked up at him. 'Leave me alone, I just got raped.'

If I expected any sympathy I was wrong. He said nothing except to demand to see my driver's license. He studied it carefully, and I suddenly felt like the guilty party.

He handed the license back to me. 'It says you are only twenty, which makes you a minor. You better come with me. We'll sort this out at the station.'

'Sort what out? Didn't you hear me I've been raped?'

He sort of shrugged his shoulders. 'Yeah, I heard you.'

It was about 3 o'clock in the morning when we arrived at the station. The cop pointed to a wooden bench and told me to sit down. I was told we were waiting for the sex squad. And I waited and waited and waited. Every time a cop walked into the station they had to pass me. Every cop that came in asked, 'Who's she?'

'Oh, that's the rape victim,' the desk sergeant would reply sarcastically without even looking up. As the time rolled on all

I wanted to do was curl up into a ball and die. It was almost like a big joke to them. But it wasn't a joke, this was the worst night of my short life. All I could think of was what Ben had done to me. That was bad enough but then when I was at my lowest point I'd been picked up, abused and raped, convinced that I was about to die. Why had this happened to me, why had G!d deserted me?

The cops came and went and I remained where I was. The same question, 'Who's she?' The same answer, the frowns and even a few sneers. I sensed in their heart of hearts they believed that the only type of woman who gets raped are the ones who ask for it.

Finally, at 6 o'clock, the sex squad showed up. Two men. Surely that couldn't be right? They were brutal. For as long as I live, I will never forget the questions they put to me. They questioned me for over an hour and in tones that told me they didn't believe me, as if I was making it all up. Were they kidding, couldn't they see the state I was in? I told them the name of the fast food place and I gave them good descriptions of both men. They didn't even bother to write it down.

'Where were you raped?'

'I don't know.'

'What do you mean you don't know?'

'I was blindfolded.'

'So, how many times did they come?'

'I don't know, I tried to block it out, everything was a blur.'

'How many times did you come?'

Were these cops crazy?

I just shut down.

They shipped me over to Washington Adventist Hospital in Takoma Park for my rape exam. More humiliation. More degradation. I was treated like a slab of meat as they probed and swabbed me while I lay almost naked on my back. I wanted to die.

Finally, I was taken back to the police station. At this point I was very close to hysteria. The cops started questioning me again.

'What were you doing with those guys? How did you know them?'

I couldn't stand it anymore. I screamed, 'I was looking to buy an overdose of heroin!'

I didn't realize it but I had just cooked my goose. If the police believe that you are suicidal or homicidal they can hold you for up to forty-eight hours for observation. They announced they were detaining me.

'Detaining me? But I'm the victim, why don't you get off your fat fucking arses and arrest these guys? I've told you where I met them, where they picked me up and what they look like, surely someone will know them.'

'You are a minor, as you are only twenty. We've called your father, he's on his way.'

My father. That stopped me. This could only get worse.

One cop was actually nice to me, he was trying to be helpful. 'Just be calm and when they question you tell them that you didn't mean what you said. Tell them you're okay now. If we sincerely believe you are suicidal we have to detain you.'

It made sense. I knew I had been stupid.

'Your father will confirm you are fine,' he continued, 'He'll have you out in no time.'

For once in my life I placed my trust in my father and couldn't wait for him to arrive. I kept looking at the clock on the station wall. What was taking him so long? After what seemed like an eternity he walked through the front door. I stood up to greet him. He glanced over to me and I thought I saw a brief warmness in his face. I was wrong. I expected a few kind words from a father, perhaps even an embrace. I was wrong. Instead he made a beeline for the desk sergeant, completely ignoring me. 'Are you in charge of Miss Kasmir?'

The sergeant looked up at him and then towards me.

'Yes sir, I am.'

My father let out a deep sigh as he shook his head. 'My daughter's been in a mental hospital. You have to watch out for her.'

My own father had condemned me before he'd even spoken to me. Any chance I had of getting out of this dilemma disappeared completely.

'She needs help,' he said. 'She needs psychiatric care.'

I lost it.

Once again he sided with the establishment people to get me locked up. I started screaming at him, calling him any hurtful names I could think of. He just stood passively and watched me.

They threw me in a cell and within the hour they were back for me. The next thing I knew I was being shoved into a patrol car and taken off to St. Elizabeths Hospital in Washington D.C. This is a mental hospital for the most vulnerable people in society.

The irony was that I was the victim and I was going to be locked up while the perpetrators went free. I became an animal. If anyone dared to approach me in those forty-eight hours I was held for observation, I literally growled at them and screamed for them to get the hell away. There was only darkness.

After forty-eight hours I was released. They made the decision that I was not suicidal after all. I went back to my father's house. When I walked through the front door he was in the living room, reading a newspaper. He glanced up. I waited for him to talk to me, I waited for him to ask how I was feeling. I waited for him to comfort me.

I got nothing.

He returned to his newspaper and I walked upstairs to my bedroom, fell on the bed and cried.

Nothing was ever said about the rape, not by my father nor the police. The police never contacted me, never followed up on the accusation, never questioned anyone at the Roy Rogers hamburger joint. Despite my injuries, my state of mind and the positive swabs for semen, the police brushed the incident under the carpet and did nothing. Two rapists were left on the streets of Washington and no one seemed to care, least of all my father.

13

When I came out of St Elizabeths Hospital I was a complete mess.

I'm honestly not sure how I survived emotionally after that. I started dabbling in all kinds of drugs, including heroin and cocaine.

The first drug I really became hooked on was speed. Mostly I would get speed by going to doctors' offices. It worked for me to complain to any quack I came across that I was fat and needed diet pills to lose weight. I'll never forget this one doctor in Takoma Park, Maryland. His waiting room looked like 14th St. Washington D.C. on a Friday night, a very seedy part of town, loaded with prostitutes and junkies. There were all kinds of sleazy-looking people in the waiting room, hanging out to get drugs. There was no pretense as to why anybody was there. People would ask each other what they were scoring. A lot of people came for painkillers but I was there for speed, usually Desoxyn. It was pharmaceutical methamphetamine.

Somewhere along the way I discovered that if you dissolved the pills in water and intravenously injected the solution, the high was much more intense.

I never stayed on any one drug for long. Usually it was just a few weeks at a time because I was so afraid I would become addicted. I didn't try to deal with my fear of addiction by not using drugs, rather I would switch onto different pills and experience a different type of high. At that time in my life I would have tried anything to get high.

I had a tall, blond and very gorgeous friend named Bill. I don't know how we met, but I'm fairly sure we were both stoned, which would explain why I couldn't remember. We became lovers immediately, and mostly we would score drugs and make love. We absolutely had the hots for each other and the sex was very tender and very intense. He was the first person I ever saw who injected himself with heroin.

We'd agreed to purchase some heroin but I assumed we were going to snort it. Even though I had injected speed, I viewed injecting heroin as in a class by itself. Bill scored the smack while I waited in his van. When we made our way back to his apartment we closed the curtains and prepared to indulge. The next thing I knew Bill whipped out a small box.

'What's that?' I asked.

'It's my kit,' he explained.

It contained a syringe, a bottle cap and a tiny piece of cotton. He said that he would cook the heroin, strain it and then pull the liquid into the syringe.

'No Bill,' I begged. 'We don't need to do that.'

He ignored me, said that I could do as I wished but this was the way he wanted to do it. After cooking up the dope, he pulled it into the syringe. Then he took off his belt, wrapped it around his bicep, pulled it tight and proceeded to take aim at the now bulging vein with the needle. I watched in horror and couldn't help bursting into tears at what I witnessed. I was so blown away and cried so much that my own hit was completely forgotten about for that moment. I watched and I cried and begged him never to do it again. He ignored my request and after about an hour realizing I wasn't getting through to him, I gave up.

It only took a month, but I went from being horrified to doing exactly the same.

Ping Pong was a friendly black guy I met that lived in the outskirts of northwest Washington D.C. I was introduced to him as someone I could trust to buy heroin from. I drove to his place, and he immediately let me in when I said my name. I told him I wanted to buy smack. He was holding and he sold me a small quantity for ninety dollars. Following the transaction, he asked me how I got high. I told him I snorted it.

He started to laugh. 'Man, what a fucking waste of money. This is good shit I'm giving you honey, and it needs to go straight into the vein.'

'No,' I said. 'No way will I ever do that.'

'You like getting high, right?'

'Sure I do.'

'So what do you like about it?'

I shrugged my shoulders.

'Just getting high I suppose.'

He laughed again. He told me to imagine the best high I'd ever had on heroin and asked me to imagine an intense one, ten times better. 'That's what you get honey. That's what you get from shooting up.'

Incredibly, despite my misgivings about shooting up heroin, I actually found myself thinking about it.

Ping Pong produced a bottle cap and a piece of wire.

'What are you doing?' I asked.

'Fixing you up, honey.'

'No, I don't want to.'

'Sure you do.'

I watched as he took my sachet of white powder, placed some of it on a spoon and mixed it with water. He cooked the heroin until it became liquid, mixed it up and handed the spoon to me.

'But I don't have any needles,' I said.

He gave me one and a cigarette filter too. I drew up the liquid into the syringe. Then I took off my belt and wrapped it around by bicep exactly the way I did for speed and completed the task by easing the needle into my vein.

Ping Pong had been right. The intensity of the high had been like nothing I had ever experienced before.

Thereafter, every morning when I woke the first thing on my mind was where my next hit was coming from. Fortunately, I couldn't afford a habit yet, that is I didn't have the money to get high every day.

14

My father felt guilty about everything that transpired, though we didn't really talk about it. He just kept quiet. I worked seven days a week as a maid and saved up to buy a secondhand 305cc Honda motorcycle. Unfortunately, the timing chain broke which rendered it useless. My father came to the rescue and bought me a 350cc Honda. I was a terror. For the few years I rode that motorcycle, I took an ambulance more than I took a taxicab. I drove like an idiot, between lanes of traffic and even up onto sidewalks at times. For a short period of time I worked as a motorcycle courier for a delivery company. When time was money, I threw all caution to the wind and drove as quickly as possible, regardless of how many stupid accidents I had. I never broke a bone though there were times I walked like a cowboy.

I will never forget the time Pam and I were riding down 16th Street in northwest Washington D.C. on a beautiful fall day. As we passed Florida Avenue, we looked to our right and an amazing house grabbed our attention. Apparently the house started life with a white rococo appearance, and someone had taken the time to paint all the trimmings in psychedelic colors. We had to stop and investigate. I parked the bike, and we walked up to the front of the house, hitting the buzzer a couple of times. A tall, well-built guy with longish brown hair answered the door. I was instantly in love. 'Hi! Couldn't help but notice your incredible house. My name is Jan and this is my best friend Pam.'

'I'm Elton. Welcome to the Florida Avenue Racing Team. That's FART for short.' This was getting better. 'Come with me downstairs to our basement and meet our mascot, Myrtle.'

We followed Elton into the house and down into a rather dark cellar. There, in the corner, was a 300-pound pig. Elton pulled out his handkerchief, and *F.A.R.T.* and a small pig were stamped on it in blue ink. 'We race dirt bikes. We take Myrtle with us whenever we go to meets.'

Elton invited us to hang out. He introduced us to his roommate, Michael, and then gave us a tour of the rest of the house.

'This is our special room' He took me to what used to be the backstairs that servants would use in a grand house. There was a platform between floors where he had installed a mattress and huge speakers, between which you could lie down. The walls were painted in fluorescent spatters and a black light made it all come alive. Unbelievable.

'I was about to do a hit of mescaline,' Elton said. 'You want some?'

Pammy and I were game. She went off with Michael and I got focused on Elton.

A couple of hours passed, and I was getting high and hot. Elton was on the same wavelength, so we started some gentle kissing. I was so taken with him I could not help but interrupt my hormonal pursuit with a lot of questions about who he was. This guy was amazing and I wanted to know everything about him.

Around that time, I thought it was amusing to quip at odd moments, 'I'm really a man'. It just seemed like a funny, stupid off-the-wall way to come back to someone after a stupid question. For instance, if someone remarked that it was unusual to see a girl driving a motorcycle I'd say, 'It's not unusual because I'm really a man', then I would laugh and they'd get the joke. Thus, when Elton said he didn't know a girl could ride a cycle, I retorted without thinking, 'That's because I'm really a man'.

I didn't think anything about the fact that he immediately seemed to slow down on the intimacy. That was actually okay because I was peaking, and wanted to pay attention to what I was seeing. We walked up to Elton's bedroom, and then he gave me a funny look. 'I need to see in your underpants.'

'What are you talking about?' I could not imagine what was going on.

'I need to see what you are working with.'

'What do you mean?' What was he thinking?

Suddenly I realized he thought I was serious about being a man. Of course. If I was peaking, he was peaking. There he was on a trip with a girl he just met and my joke about being a man scared him to death. 'You poor sweetheart! I must have scared the shit out of you. I was only joking about being a man. I absolutely have a pussy.'

'Can you show me?' he said, rather sheepishly.

'No worries! You can taste it as well if you want to.'

Fortunately, that seemed to clear everything up.

I never did get to see them race, though Elton would stop by my house on occasion for great sex.

My motorcycle gave me a great sense of freedom. I loved breaking out of gender expectations. A few times I drove much bigger bikes just to prove I could.

That summer a young physician friend of mine went to Woods Hole, Massachusetts to study, and he left me with his townhouse. Dan was very unusual for a doctor. He had graduated from Harvard, though I really knew nothing more about his medical credentials. He had shared with me he was on the diving team at college.

My favorite story he shared involved a husband and wife psychiatrist who were his friends at Harvard. It seems the husband made a batch of LSD and they both tried it. Almost immediately they both started having a bad trip. Because he feared that LSD was chemically close to ergotamine poison, they both started freaking out that their health might be in danger.

'Get me help!' his wife shouted.

'Help, help, help' he called out feebly. That was his way of getting 'help'.

They ended up admitting themselves to the hospital and all was well.

So, there I was with this great townhouse. It was about midnight when I drove to Wisconsin Avenue to an all-night place to get breakfast. As soon as I pulled my bike up in front of the cafe, four gorgeous customized Harley Davidson motorcycles came roaring up to the curb. We all entered the place together and immediately began to talk.

I cut to the chase, 'You guys need a place to stay?'

'Sure!' They replied in unison.

'After we eat, follow me!'

They were really a nice bunch of guys. Jerry was the son of a dentist and Ralph was a truck driver. The other two guys, Vince and Bob never really shared what they did, but these were not thugs. They were all visiting from Levittown, Pennsylvania.

Ralph and I hit it off. He was just my type, tall, dark with a beard and a very hot body. He and I shared the master bedroom, while the others made do. He was a stud, and I'm sure we kept the others awake with all the screaming and fucking.

The next day we decided to go out for a run, and *I got to be leader of the pack*! I couldn't have been more thrilled. There I was at the head, leading these gorgeous bikes with matching hot bikers. I had died and gone to heaven.

The highlight for me was when we had stopped at a light. A guy next to me in a sports car gave me a dirty look. They didn't miss it. They started leaning on their horns and looked positively menacing. I knew at that moment I was well looked after. I never felt so special in my life.

They had to leave too soon, but I would make several trips to Levittown to visit. I was always welcome.

My cycle did a great deal to bolster my sense of self. I honestly felt tough, like no one could mess with me. When it got a bit cool I would wear an insulated jacket and pants that would cover me from head to foot. I remember after getting off my bike, as I just stood, some wise guy randomly screamed at me, 'Hey! Are you a boy or a girl?'

'What do you think?' I yelled back.

'Suck my dick!'

Yup. Attitude.

15

I needed to escape from the drug scene or it would have killed me. I knew the dealers and where they lived and all my money went on heroin. I was spiraling out of control and I knew it. I knew it but could do nothing about it.

One day I got the break I was looking for. It felt like G!d was looking out for me. Pam had hung in with her schooling and graduated from George Washington University with a bachelor's degree. I was so happy for her. She announced a few days after graduation that her parents had given her $2000 as a graduation present - a huge sum in those days, and she decided to spend it on the trip to Europe.

'Wow, that's fabulous,' I said, really pleased for her as she sat with a big grin on her face while telling me all about it.

'And you're coming with me?'

'I don't have enough money.'

She wouldn't take no for an answer and said she wasn't going anywhere without her best friend.

'If you won't come, then I'm staying here too.'

I hugged her. 'Okay, I'm in.'

I scraped together every penny I could over the next month and we planned our great adventure. We booked tickets into Lisbon, Portugal. Off we went on that long flight. I took a bunch of pills so that I could try and sleep the trip away, and when we arrived I was extremely groggy and barely coherent. When we got off the plane we found a cab driver, handed him the name of the hotel and miraculously arrived intact. We were so exhausted that we dragged our suitcases into the room and crawled into bed. I absolutely had to go to the bathroom. We had not booked rooms with a bathroom, so I was completely surprised to find a toilet in our room. I was greatly relieved because I thought I was going to explode. I honestly did not feel like I could manage trying to find a bathroom in the hotel so I was grateful they had made a mistake and gave us a room with the toilet.

When I awoke the next day, I started rethinking our toilet. I remembered reading Henry Miller's *Tropic of Cancer* and *Tropic of Capricorn*. One of those books had a story about a sailor who was hanging out with French whores. He used a bidet to take a shit and when one of the whores discovered the turd floating in the bidet she threw the soldier out, calling him a pig.

It dawned on me that the toilet I used was most probably a bidet. Lesson learned.

We were in Lisbon for less than a day. It was industrial and dingy, and held no appeal. We decided to get out of there as quickly as possible. We heard about the Algarve before we left the States. We promised we would get there as quickly as possible as it was supposed to be heavenly. So, we packed up our suitcases and headed to the Algarve, the coastal region.

We found the landscape to be very dramatic. It was all cliffs and beaches with a beautiful blue ocean. It was absolutely glorious. Almost immediately we met two guys, Antonio and Eugene, and hooked up for our time in Portugal. Eugene was tall and thin, with dark hair and bright blue eyes. He was my age and spoke no English. Antonio was about the same age, with light brown hair and slightly heavier built. Again, no English, but as long as we had our Berlitz book we could communicate. They had nothing better to do than hang out with us. We had an amazing time with these guys; drinking, making love, swimming, and tanning.

One day Eugene took us to his village to see a dance. The little town was so quaint. No doubt the whole village had turned out for the event. Entire families were sitting on benches, watching while the pretty young girls in party dresses were danced about by the young men dressed in their finest suits. I noticed that every move was carefully watched by mothers, grandmothers, fathers and grandfathers. Us American girls drew quite a few stares too. The music was provided by local musicians and the entire affair was very lively and charming.

Afterwards Eugene took me to his house. It was a small cottage with a dirt floor. In the eating area was a large wooden bowl used for making bread. Eugene's room was tiny, and scantily furnished with just a bed and a small table. There was a small red plastic transistor radio on the table.

There really wasn't much to do, so we went back to my hotel room in a cab. I couldn't believe how impoverished he and his family were. They owned practically nothing and it shocked me. He was a very handsome young man, and I couldn't imagine the kind of life he led.

What a love affair, I spoke no Portuguese and he spoke no English. My Berlitz book allowed me to figure out a few phrases, so we were able to communicate a little bit, but I really could not get into his head. Mostly we didn't need to speak, we just made love and we enjoyed being in each other's company. It worked well and we laughed at the awkwardness of it all.

One day we all decided to rent horses and spent a few hours atop some pretty wild creatures. My horse had an unfortunate tendency to buck. The thought of getting thrown off the horse absolutely terrified me. Pammy's horse was somewhat tamer and we managed to survive the adventure in one piece. It was actually quite a thrill to be on horseback in the meadows and pastures of the Algarve.

One morning Pam came to me, looking rather sheepish and embarrassed. She had been sleeping with Antonio that night and told me what had happened: when they slept together, he hogged the whole bed. Eventually through the course of the evening and early morning poor Pammy got pushed further and further towards the wall of the room until she found herself squashed into a small space. Finally, she could stand it no longer. She snapped.

'Antonio! Enough!' She was yelling. They were both naked in bed of course and it worked, Pam got his attention. He woke up and sat up next to her. 'Nada para me,' she fumbled through an explanation in extremely limited Portuguese mixed with English, trying to explain their spatial arrangements with gestures.

'This is para me,' she yelled, slamming her fist down on the bed next to her, 'and this is para you!' She reached over to slam her fist down on the space next to him. Unfortunately for Antonio it was quite dark and Pam miscalculated her aim. She slammed her clenched fist down on what she thought was his side of the bed, missed and caught him right in the balls.

Poor Antonio. Pam said she thought he was going to die, it was some seconds before he even managed to breathe but eventually he let out a painful, low moan, whimpering softly with the most pitiful expression of complete agony mixed with humiliation.

'Nada para me,' he cried and slid slowly to the floor in a heap. He did not move for quite some time, thinking that this was Pammy's way of bringing their sexual relationship to a close.

The beautiful boys and our wonderful time on the Algarve was nearing the end. We were limited by language, but we were able to make them understand it was time for us to move on.

We found a train station and booked a trip through Spain stopping off in Madrid on the way to Barcelona.

Most of our time in Madrid was spent in pursuit of culture. We visited the Prado museum, such an incredible collection of Goya, El Greco, Dali and Picasso. We hooked up with a guy who turned us on to a cheap restaurant. We lived on chicken and rice and wine, pollo y arroz and vino. Later we learned that we had been eating at a Cuban restaurant, never getting an idea of what native Spanish food tasted like. Oh well, it was certainly cheap, less than a few dollars per meal, and tasted great.

In Spain one of the culinary differences we noticed had to do with the bread. It was dense and pasty, made from bleached flour and not very tasty. No crust to speak of. In fact, as we went from country to country we noticed that the bread changed greatly in character. Spanish bread was a bust for me, bland with almost no taste, the crust was soft and had no bite or crunch to it. When we got to Paris, we found bread that was to die for.

At one point near Barcelona we took a small ferry boat down the coast. It seemed mostly to carry locals with a few tourists who were easily spotted. An old woman in her late seventies, completely covered in black, moved from person to person begging. Pammy reached into her purse and pulled out a one-dollar bill and gave it to the old lady as we had run out of Spanish currency, and we thought U.S. dollars were accepted almost anywhere. The woman looked puzzled and walked across the boat to a small group of older women. The old woman showed them the dollar bill Pam had given her, and there was much humming and frowns as they all appeared to inspect it. Finally, the woman seem to realize that she had been given American money and a rather substantial amount, too. She gave a toothless grin and waved back at us. Pam acknowledged the woman's triumph by giving her a sign. Pam's intention was to convey 'Right on'. I think she had seen the sign repeated several times in Portugal and did her best to replicate what she thought was a term of endearment; she shoved her fist high into the air and at the same time gripped her bicep with her other hand. Oh dear. It turned out to be the

European sign for 'Fuck you!'. The old woman looked stunned and the other old ladies mortified. The remainder of the voyage proceeded in stony silence with an occasional glare from the old Spanish ladies. It wasn't until later, when Pam attempted to do the same gesture again, that some guy explained to her what it really meant. She was absolutely horrified. Oh well, live and learn.

The rest of our time in Spain was uneventful. No guys and absolutely no getting high on drugs, just wine.

From Spain we took a train to Paris.

We booked a sleeper car that we shared with a young married German couple. The husband was absolutely adorable. My comments and observations were not kept to myself. While they chatted away in German, I made remarks about how incredibly edible I thought he was. Nice hair, cute smile, a great butt and what I'd like to do to him given half a chance.

'So cute,' said Pammy.

'Cute doesn't even go there,' I said. 'I'd fuck him to heaven and back.'

We drank French wine and our comments got naughtier and naughtier as we giggled like little schoolgirls. Eventually it was time for bed and using hand signals we indicated to our German travel companions that we were tired. Our couchette seats turned into beds and as we stood, the gorgeous specimen flipped the seats for us. I made more comments on what I was going to do with his manhood once the lights went out. I felt perfectly safe that all my filthy comments were not being understood. We laughed and giggled until eventually we fell asleep. In the morning, an hour or two from Paris, the daylight streamed through the window and we all gradually awoke. As the German hunk stood and stretched and rubbed the night sleep from his eyes, his wife turned to her husband and said in perfect English, 'Darling, will you please open the window?'.

At that point, realizing that every lewd comment I made about the husband was perfectly understood. I contemplated hurling myself from the train to avoid further embarrassment. Truly, I wanted to die.

I turned to the husband. 'You speak English?'

'Fluently,' he replied. 'My wife too.'

At the journey's end, Gare du Nord, I quietly walked away. I have never been so embarrassed in my life.

The Paris bakeries were unbelievable. We were hungry and stopped at a small patisserie just outside the station. The smell hit us as soon as we walked through the elegant doorway. Not only was the bread to die for, crusty and flavorful, but every single bit of pastry was an adventure. I knew that if I stayed in France for too long I would double in weight in no time.

In Paris we met Philip and Gregory who were traveling together. Philip was around my age, a Brit, just a little bit taller than me with sandy, curly hair and a cute body. I hooked up with him briefly but we only lasted a week as a couple.

Gregory was at least ten years older than us with horrible bucked teeth. He was tall with collar length, straight black hair. He had no style at all and he was undoubtedly the brains in that pair. In fact, he seemed to take charge of all four of us, becoming a sort of father figure to us. It seemed like we instantly became a team and pooled our energy and resources.

One night we mentioned the fact that we had to be careful with our money as we were running a little low. Gregory told us not to worry and explained to us how to get money by defrauding American Express. It was a very simple scheme. We bought traveler's checks and then claimed that they had been lost. We sat tight for a few days and, sure enough, American Express replaced the missing checks, which of course were still in our handbags. Good old AmEx. In time we then proceeded to spend the new and the old checks, making sure that nobody ever asked us for any identification. It was so simple and we repeated the exercise two or three times. We scammed over $300. We never detected any sign of trouble while in Europe.

With plenty money in our pockets we took a train from Paris to Amsterdam. By this time Pam and Phil were an item. They seemed very happy together and it didn't bother me in the slightest.

During our time in Spain and in France we had been extremely careful not to use any illegal drugs. The State Department in the U.S. had made a concerted effort to alert the youth traveling abroad about the dangers of getting busted with illegal drugs. The penalties were severe, the prisons were hell holes. We were terrified so we used nothing illegal. Wine was fine. In Spain we managed to find a legal over-the-counter drug that sounded like Bustaid - it was a diet pill that turned out to be a pretty good buzz. As long as we weren't breaking any laws we were satisfied.

Of course, when we arrived in Amsterdam we knew everything changed. We had arrived in Nirvana. We could not believe the differences in attitude. Everything we wanted to get high was available. The cops had long hair and they were actually very nice. It was unimaginable. My experiences with the U.S. cops were like dealing with Nazis. Thinking back, especially to the protests in Georgetown where they had physically attacked us, we referred to them as pigs because no other description fit as well. No one in Holland would ever think to use the word pig to refer to these wonderful cops. These were gentle beings.

Almost immediately we scored some hashish and some acid. It was a piss to find drugs. Marijuana did not seem to be available anywhere. Instead, everyone seemed to smoke hashish.

My first night tripping was fabulous, everything looked like Van Gogh had painted it. I looked up in the moonlit sky and saw energy lines, encircling the yellow ball that was the moon. I realized that Van Gogh must have painted what he saw. The energy lines emanated from everything. Nothing was static. It was pure magic.

We went to the Paradiso, a government run club that had music and lights and, above all, hashish. As you approached the place, people came up to you trying to sell their stuff, 'hash, hash, two guilders a gram'.

When we entered the building there were stairs on either side that climbed up to an elegant landing. On the landing there was a boutique that sold clothing and jewelry and other beautiful objects. After looking around and spending some time there we made our way back downstairs to another large area where people were dancing. The music was wonderful and the walls were covered with an amazing psychedelic light show. It was like nothing we had ever seen before. There was a stage where one young man danced solo. It seemed like the right thing to do so I hopped up and joined him, undulating and becoming one with the music and the lights and the energy. I danced until I dropped. It was hot and I was sweating. I jumped down and found Pam, it was time to get high. We asked around and were told to go upstairs. When we reached the stairs at the top, the areas were divided. In the first area people were smoking chillums, a cone shaped clay smoking apparatus filled with hash, while playing chess. In the second area people did not pretend that there was anything else happening but getting stoned, so you could just sit on the bench and puff until you were ready to pass out.

It was all magic. I honestly wished I could stay in Holland forever.

However, it wasn't to be, because we were running low on money. I started to get scared and wanted to go home. The thought of being stranded thousands of miles from home with no means to get back really worried me. Other girls could simply mail their parents and flight tickets would be booked or money wired. It was not possible for me to do that.

I sat down one night with Pam and the boys and explained it was time for me to go. She tried to talk me out of it but I'd made my mind up.

Greg got me a return ticket that flew me home via Düsseldorf, Germany. Pam was madly in love with Phillip at this point so she decided to stay. I kissed and hugged her goodbye, she looked so very happy and I thanked her for sharing the experience of a lifetime with me. It wasn't more than a few weeks later she was in a terrible motorcycle accident in Germany with Phillip. They were on the autobahn where there was no speed limit and it was a wonder she wasn't killed on the motorcycle, as they were travelling at an extremely high speed. The accident was bad enough though, she was catapulted from the bike and thrown into the autobahn wall where her leg took the brunt of the impact. Her leg was severely broken, necessitating surgery. Throughout her ordeal in Mettman Hospital, Germany, Phillip stayed by her side. When she was released from the hospital she travelled with Phillip back to northern England where he lived, and stayed with his family for a few weeks. They were married in a civil ceremony in the U.K. Some weeks later, they returned to the States and lived with her parents in Bethesda, Maryland.

16

I was back in the United States once again. The high of the European adventure was hard to come down from. Although I had to come home, part of me wished I was back in Holland, and in particular Amsterdam. The reality of what I had come back to hit me hard. There was so much uncertainty in my life. I had no profession and no special qualifications that made a good job possible. Worse than that, I had no real aspirations, no burning ambition. I had to work to support myself and of course fund the drug abuse that I knew I would slip back into.

I was on familiar terrain again and I knew where to score anything I wanted. I mostly worked waitressing, but that was completely uninspiring and I felt myself slipping into that all familiar depression once again. I did seem to have a little bit of excitement when I landed a job as a cocktail waitress at the Shoreham Americana. The Shoreham used to be a glamorous residential hotel in its heyday and was really quite famous. I figured if I was destined to serve food and drink to people then it might as well be somewhere like this. I had only served food before, never alcohol, but they needed a cocktail waitress so I fudged my way through the interview, lied my ass off and landed the job.

As I was never really much of a drinker it was very tough for me in the beginning. I just did not recognize what people were asking for. I'll never forget my first order: The guy wanted a Dewar's and water. Dewar's is a very classy brand of scotch though I didn't know that. I had him repeat the order several times and finally wrote down D-O-O-R-S. Fortunately, the bartender knew exactly what I was talking about so with a huge slice of luck I delivered the right drink.

The bartender actually took me under his wing, guiding me to the right glass for each drink. He was a tall, dark, Persian man with a big belly and always had a rough, stubbly face. And he had an ulcer. He was always drinking cream to sooth the burning in his gut. When he wasn't pouring drinks, he was studying which I sincerely admired. A lot of Persians came to America to attend college. My bartending friend wanted to become an engineer.

Featured at the hotel was a revival of Minsky's Follies, a girlie show with song and dance. This was all very exciting as it featured bare-breasted dancers. The all-male staff of Spanish waiters had never seen anything like this. They would stand in the kitchen and look through the small window in the door trying to get a glimpse of a bare breast or two. The purpose of this window was so that a waiter could be seen coming through the door and avoid crashing into the waiter who was exiting through the door. Unfortunately, management got tired of the staff standing at the door and peeking out so they put paper over the window to block the view. It was a complete disaster. It meant the waiters could no longer see the bare breasts or the waiter coming through the door! They began crashing into each other constantly. After several hundred dollars' worth of broken dishes and ruined meals the paper was finally removed from the windows and management just had to live with it.

The money was good, with New Year's Eve producing an unbelievable night. My partner and I ended up making over $400 each in tips, (that's over $3800 in today's money), and I did not make one single mistake. My waiter partner, Jimmy, carried plates stacked a mile high and served the revelers with incredible precision.

At the hotel, I became friends with an older woman, Hilda. She was a bartender who worked in the lobby area. She was a small German woman with chin length blond hair curled under in a pageboy cut, with fairly obvious facial plastic surgery. She was so vain and unsuccessfully attempted to hide her age. Even with a facelift she pretty much looked her sixty-plus years. I am sure it would have crushed her if I ever hinted she looked her age. Poor Hilda spent most of her time lusting after a musician that played the bass in the Follies show. He was at least twenty-five years her junior.

I did like her despite her obvious shortcomings and we slowly but surely became good friends. Usually, we would chat a bit between drink orders. Finally, one night she invited me over to her apartment which was on Connecticut Avenue, near the hotel.

It was a short walk, up a flight of stairs to her small one-bedroom apartment. She had furnished it pleasantly with old stuff that had seen better days, not really antiques, just old. Things were kind of frilly and fussy and definitely popular during a different era, but just not working now.

Hilda started to tell me about her incredible past that was intertwined with Shoreham Americana's history. She'd been a cigarette girl back in the fifties. Her husband, Paul Du Meyer, was the orchestra leader. His group played out on the terrace of the Palladium Room. She described how he would be completely drunk by the end of each night and then somehow he would make his way home and into their bedroom. Very carefully he would drape his tuxedo over the chair and then fall into bed, dead drunk. The next day he would wake up fine and start his entire routine over. Work, drunk then collapse into bed.

He died some years before I ever met Hilda. She pulled out an album of old pictures. She showed me the beautiful dresses the hotel would let her buy for her role as a cigarette girl. They would give her $300 which was an incredible sum of money back in the fifties and take her go to a place like Lord and Taylor to buy her a very fancy dress. She would walk around the dinner tables and hotel lobby with a tray holding cigarettes and add atmosphere to each room. After her husband died she took up bartending because the cigarette girl role lost its popularity and was eventually done away with. It was obvious that a little bit of Hilda died with the demise of the cigarette girl.

Hilda told me that she was going to have another facelift. In her mid-sixties? She had already had her breasts done by a surgeon whose nickname was 'The G!d'. I was fascinated as she described the process and how magnificent her breasts felt afterwards. I'd never had anything but a flat chest my entire life. I was always very self-conscious about the fact that I wore an AA bra. I was five foot eight and kind of medium weight and always felt self-conscious about not having a great bust. I endlessly endured stupid jokes, like having someone point to my bust, saying, 'A little Clearasil will take care of that'. My curiosity was aroused.

The other friend I made at the hotel was Paul, who worked in the lunchroom as a waiter. His passion was doing drag shows where he dressed up in full makeup and costume and went by the name Sophie Tucker. He/She was a drag queen and proceeded to enlighten me about the transvestite scene in Washington. He explained there were competitions such as the Miss Gay USA, and then there were entertainment venues. It so happened the entertaining drag show, *The Hottest Ticket in Town*, was taking place in a few weeks. This was a show put on by a group of local queens, who all worked incredibly hard to create an amazing production. In fact, if I would like to be in the show, I was welcome! They planned to introduce a girl into their stage show to provide a twist to the evening. The audience would be invited to guess who the real girl was. It was certainly different and I was up for it.

The first rehearsal night was frightening. I was very shy about speaking to these people and was quite hopeful they would accept me as a friend. I worried that climbing on stage with them might be a problem as they might resent me for being a real girl. I put my anxiety on hold and showed up ready for the first rehearsal.

I was introduced, and tried to nonchalantly hang out while some of the queens were getting dressed. At first some of the queens started making crude remarks about taping their penises. 'Girlfriend,' one queen blurted out, 'my dick is so sore from ripping off tape after each of these damn rehearsals that I'm gonna have to wear soft gloves when I hold myself to piss.'

I got more and more nervous by the second and at one point one of them even taped his penis up right in front of me.

It didn't take long for the tension to ease because I played it cool. Once they became used to my presence they all seemed to really like me. One asked me if I knew how to do a show walk and I had to admit I was completely clueless.

'Don't worry honey, we'll teach you in no time.'

Everybody had a good time getting into the act, the queens doing their best show walk before encouraging me to mimic them. Fortunately, I had studied dance when I was younger and could move quite well.

'Fucking hell, the bitch has the rhythm of a black dude!' The queens really started to like me

Within thirty minutes I had the show walk down pat.

All the music was taken from *A Chorus Line*. I was going to be in the number where each of us represented a month of the year. I was going to be July. We decided that I should be Aunt Sam, coinciding with Independence Day, decked out in something red, white and blue. So, I proceeded to plan my costume. I thought I was going to be amazing and really looked forward to showing the guys what I could do and how good I could look. The next day I went to a fabric store and bought sequins and material. I was extremely excited. I even found a top hat that I could decorate, which I ended up covering in glue and then sprinkling red, white and blue glitter all over it.

So, on dress rehearsal night everybody showed up with their costumes. I thought I was going to be an amazing hit. I was nervous so decided that smoking a little pot would settle me down. I had on sequin-trimmed short-shorts and a tailcoat that I had trimmed with sequins, all red, white and blue. I had my sparkly glittered top hat on, which I thought was the bomb. As the queens showed up one by one I became crestfallen. I realized I was a hen among peacocks.

I didn't perform well. Probably because I was stoned. However, as I looked around to behold the incredible costumes I felt like Alice in Wonderland. I was in awe of the phenomenal colors and the glitz of it all. I started to bum when I saw my reflection. I felt like a big nothing. The queens were so amazing and clearly I wasn't.

Chita Rivera came up to me and said, 'Don't despair darling. We will fix you up.' Chita was known as the tulle queen, in that she loved to use very flimsy, gauzy materials and just frilled the hell out of everything. 'Now darling, we can fix this! Just do as I tell you to do. What you need to buy is three yards of red tulle, three yards of blue tulle and three yards of white. Then I want you to buy everything else on this list. Don't worry darling, you are going to be fabulous. You are at a good starting point and once you feel special it will all come together.'

I was so envious of them. All I wanted to do was to be a part of the group and feel their special, fabulous nature. There was so much glamour and so much elegance and I wanted to feel that I was a part of that. They all seemed so confident, so relaxed, so sure and clear as if they knew exactly what to do. I envied them their self-confidence.

The next day I ran to the fabric store as soon as I got up and bought everything that Chita had instructed me to get. I did not skimp on anything. We had agreed that I would come over to Chita's place and that she would help me sew all the stuff up into a fabulous costume.

When I got to her place I met her roommate, Stanley. He was a nice-looking young man, a little quieter than Chita but still definitely a show queen. He quickly walked me back to his closet crammed full of show costumes. Meanwhile, Chita grabbed all my purchases and immediately began to sew for hours, creating an amazing costume for me. Truly, I felt like one of them. She whipped a costume together like a professional seamstress. She was nothing short of amazing to watch.

Eventually, when she was finished, she stood up. 'I need to pick up a few finishing touches, so I've got to run out to the store. I'm not gonna be back for about an hour. You kids have fun while I'm gone.'

I wasn't sure what that was supposed to mean. She had a strange smile on her face as she walked out of the door. Stanley and I went into the living room. The place was kind of small and nondescript. You'd never believe that a couple of glamorous show queens lived there. It was all pretty sedate, kind of like any person's home, middle-class, not a lot of money, nothing special.

Conservative.

I asked Stanley how he got into this whole business but he didn't seem interested in talking about it. 'How long have you been a show queen?'

He shrugged his shoulders. 'I have just been doing it a couple years.'

I persisted. 'Have you and Chita been friends for a long time?'

Eventually he opened up a little. 'Yes,' he laughed. 'Actually, I used to go to school with Chita, back as far as junior high school. We were never really close, though we did use to enjoy playing with dolls together. That was our big secret.'

I laughed too. 'Well I guess you've come a long way since playing with dolls?'

I wanted to take it back. What a stupid thing to say but he didn't seem to mind. Something was drawing me to get to the bottom of these queen's relationship but Stanley wasn't giving much away. 'Do you have a boyfriend, Stanley, or a girlfriend even?'

Boy, I thought, this is getting worse. I just did not know what to say. How do you get to the bottom of someone's sexuality when you've only known them for a couple of hours? I knew that both Stanley and Chita were transvestites, but I had never actually seen them together. Yet they shared an apartment, and who knows, possibly a bed too.

While I was thinking of something else to say he came straight out with it.

'I've never actually been with a woman before.'

There was an awkward silence as he appeared to hang his head. Now I was interested. This gorgeous twenty-something man had never been with a girl. He was a virgin!

'You were never attracted to women? Did you only like guys?'

He looked up. 'I don't think I ever liked girls and yet I don't dislike them in that way. I look at pretty girls like the next man but don't think of them in a sexual way.'

I couldn't even believe what I was saying but I couldn't stop myself. 'How can you knock something if you've never tried it?' I leaned forward instinctively and kissed him on the lips. He immediately got into it, moving his lips in conjunction with mine while his tongue probed my mouth. Stanley was very attractive. He was my height, with dark hair and bright blue eyes and very soft lips. I found him very sexy.

I stood up and took his hand. 'Where is your bedroom?'

He pointed over to a corridor and led me to his bedroom. He was very slow and sensitive about taking off my clothes. I reciprocated and undressed him completely. He slowly started kissing me from head to toe. I didn't get the sense that he had never been around a woman's body because he was certainly turning me on. He knew how to touch me softly but in a stimulating, sexy way. I was getting really hot as he pushed me gently onto the bed and by the time he penetrated me I was wet and ready.

We made love twice. It seemed he couldn't get enough of me and then we heard the front door open.

'Oh shit, it's Chita,' I whispered.

'Hello girls, are you home? Are you here? What's going on?'

We heard her walking around the lounge. I didn't even think about the fact that she and Stanley might be together. Holy shit. I'm going to get myself killed. I heard her approaching the bedroom door.

'Are you in here?'

This is it. She'll explode, reach for the nearest weapon and slaughter us both in the bed.

Chita walked in. 'I'm sorry,' I stuttered, I was about to beg forgiveness and for my life. She just smiled.

'You girls better be careful not to get pregnant.' She turned and walked away, laughing her head off. I was mortified as I rushed around to get my clothes back on. Stanley and I walked sheepishly out of the bedroom back to the lounge.

Chita sat on a chair rummaging in one of the bags she had just bought.

'If you two girls are quite finished, let's get back to business. Let's get on with finishing up this fitting or we won't have a show.'

The rest of the afternoon was spent sewing. Stanley quickly ducked out, saying he had to go to work and that was the last I saw of him until the night of the final dress rehearsal.

The show was a complete success. Barely anybody could guess who the real girl was. I don't know if that said more about them or me. My little flat chest had two sequence stars, one covering each nipple. Over that I had a red white and blue tailcoat. My top hat was wrapped with red, white and blue tulle and saturated with sparkling glitter. I had tap shoes on that were encased in glitter too. I felt like a rock star. The night went off without a hitch and I loved every second. I was proud of myself.

17

Although I loved my time at The Shoreham Americana I knew it wasn't the long-term prospect I wanted. I left and managed to get a few jobs working as a clerk in various health food stores. I don't know exactly what it was that pulled me to this type of environment but I enjoyed working there more than just waitressing. I was poorly paid but it was a pleasant environment with a more upmarket clientele as the health foods were awfully expensive. I enjoyed having access to the health foods through the store and as I was working long hours it only seemed fair to eat some of it. It didn't feel like stealing. After all, there was no way I could afford to buy this stuff on what they were paying me. I felt my work deserved to be rewarded so I helped myself to the food.

One day I was having lunch, courtesy of the shop, when I saw a job advertised in the *Washington Post* for a residential counselor. I started to think. Could I become a counselor? Why not? I had been in a lot of therapy and knew the difference between a good counselor and a bad one. Believe me, I had seen both types of counselors. The more I thought about it the more I thought I could do the job. I had the confidence that I could listen to other peoples' problems the way good therapists listened to mine. That was key, listen and let people share their unhappiness with you. I applied within the hour and was more than happy when, a few days later, I was told to come in for an interview.

When I arrived at my job interview at The Boys and Girls Home of Montgomery County, I learned that they were looking for a live-in counselor. Even better. The interview went very well. I was in my element describing to the interviewer exactly how I would conduct myself with the girls in my care. Towards the end of the interview I saw my interviewer smiling and nodding her head in agreement. I had the job; I could feel it in my bones. Sure enough when we finished the interview she asked me how soon I could start.

Each shift was twenty-four hours. The counselors shared a little bedroom which offered limited privacy but that was okay. Our meals were shared in a communal dining room. It was great and I knew I was going to fit in. The house was large enough to accommodate the three girls' counselors comfortably. The home had a nice back yard where we could sit and talk and drink coffee. All in all, things were very pleasant.

We had a wonderful psychologist, Dr. Sam, who would meet with the counselors and then the girl residents separately, at least once a week. The girls went through their therapy sessions with just the psychologist. The counselors attended sessions with just the psychologist to try to work on making the house run smoothly. Dr. Sam was truly knowledgeable, very personable and helpful to everybody. Although I was more than confident in my role as a counselor after everything I'd been through, Dr. Sam helped me to see I had a lot more to learn. I will never forget one of the most outstanding concepts he taught me. He said to never mistake rejection for failure. I will carry that thought to my grave.

Dr. Sam was great but the director of the organization wasn't. She was completely clueless about her role and she took her insecurity out on the counselors. I honestly felt she had little time or real concern for the girls. Mostly she hid in her office or was away from the home. I recall one day how she seemed to be hung up on getting the girls to play badminton. I don't know why. None of the girls even wanted to play, it just wasn't their thing. It seemed her own personal fantasy to turn them into polite middle-class girls. Perhaps something she could write in one of her reports. She was giving the girls all the rules and extolling the virtues of taking up a nice gentle sport but all they really wanted to do was to play pool, smoke a cigarette or just talk.

Unfortunately, I developed into an unofficial spokesperson for the staff, standing up for everything we felt was wrong with the way the director ran the home. I felt good about standing up for what I believed to be right, but this all proved to be a huge liability. Generally, I became the target for her anger and frustration. She called me into the office one day and told me to take a back seat or I would regret it. I tried to reason with her, saying that I was only trying to ensure a smooth running of the home, which was everyone's ultimate goal. But it was her way or no way and she wouldn't have it. She told me that I was the least experienced of all the counselors and had no right to tell her how to run things. I told her that if we felt something was wrong or wasn't running right it was my duty to tell her. She was fuming. As I walked from the office I sensed my days were numbered. I was right. Within a few weeks I was dismissed over some small non-issue. It was so insignificant that I can't even recall what it was. I was very hurt, because I knew that for once I had found a job where I could make a difference. The director was incredibly disconnected from the counselors and the girls, and if she had only listened to some of our suggestions and criticisms the place would have been a whole lot better. I can honestly say that everything I proposed was for the benefit of the troubled girls in there. When word got out that I was fired, the girls were terribly upset and one or two of my fellow counselors were in tears. There was an atmosphere of disbelief and anger. A few girls stood around just outside of the director's office. The director stepped from her office, walked right up to me, looked me in the eye and said, 'What are you doing on the premises? I told you to clear your things out and go.' She looked at her watch. 'I'll give you another thirty minutes.'

That was it. No change of heart, no second chance.

I went home and immediately called Dr. Sam. He hadn't been on duty at the time. I told him what had happened. He said that he would be happy to meet with me to try and help me get through the anguish over losing my job. He would also try and reason with the director but didn't sound too hopeful. He came over to my apartment very quickly.

Unfortunately, his agenda included comforting me by getting me into bed. I honestly had never even thought about him sexually. That really wasn't what I needed at that moment. What I wanted was comfort and kind understanding. But, he came in and gave me a hug. I guess I lingered in his arms a little longer than was necessary. Before I knew it he was kissing me passionately.

I pulled away from him. 'No Ron, stop it. It's not right, you know it's not right.'

He came for me again and I succumbed. I always did. I could never tell the difference between a man who wanted me for who I really was or someone who just wanted my body, just using me for nothing more than a quick fuck. I succumbed because I wanted to be wanted and loved. Not just fucked and forgotten.

What I got from Dr. Sam was being seduced and used for a quick fuck. He was married so I knew this wasn't the beginning of a wonderful romance and he was at least twenty years older than me. He was in fact a great disappointment. I had looked up to this man in every aspect of his work, in particularly his professionalism, and in the space of less than an hour he had destroyed it all.

I went through several days of depression. It seemed that the universe was conspiring to break me. The horrific events that had occurred in my short life were mounting. Even though I had only lost a job, it was monumental to me as I had been happy. I loved that it was full-time and live-in as it meant I couldn't go and score and get wasted. Full-time employment in a satisfying job was a great way to kick a drug habit.

I stayed away from dope less than a week.

I picked up the phone and dialed the number.

'Hi Ping Pong, it's Jan.'

'Hey Jan.'

'You got some decent junk over there?'

'Sure have, honey.'

'Great, I'll be right over.'

I picked up a belt and my kit and left for downtown Washington.

I got high only that once. I wanted to fight and conquer this demon. I was hung up on the fact I had been fired but remembered Dr. Sam's words about rejection and failure. I had been a good counselor and I knew it. Despite the cutting comments and vitriol the director had thrown at me, I knew I had been professional and as good as any other counselor. More than one of the girls had told me so, and the counselors echoed that sentiment, too. I immediately replied to an advertisement for another counseling position I saw in the newspaper. Incidentally, it turned out the director was fired from her position within the month after I left.

The Prince George's County health department was looking for counselors. I knew I could do it. I didn't have any schooling or degrees but by virtue of the fact I had been in so much therapy for drug abuse myself, I knew I could land the job and be a good counselor so I went ahead and applied.

Mr. Thomas B. Drummond was the person who interviewed me. This was a methadone clinic that the county health department ran. Methadone is a synthetic opioid, a heroin substitute that takes away the craving for the drug. I knew I could relate to the people coming in, and I sincerely wanted to help. I explained my earnest desire to help and the value of my experience with drugs to Mr. Drummond, and he seemed pleased. The interview went well. He called me within the week to offer me the job.

I was introduced almost immediately to a guy named Stuart who was already working there. Mr. Drummond had explained before we met him that Stuart was an ex-junkie turned counselor. I think Stuart was very depressed and in time I witnessed him drinking on duty. I knew that he drank quite a bit but at the time I didn't really see any connection between drinking and drugs, so the fact he boozed didn't bother me.

I really loved working at the clinic. I spent half an hour with each person listening to their wishes and hopes and dreams. I did everything I could to try and help them stay on the straight and narrow. I was inspired to try to improve myself. I liked how it felt when I told people I was a counselor.

I desperately wanted to change how I looked, as I was almost two-hundred pounds. I joined Weight Watchers and over the course of ten months I lost almost seventy-five pounds. Unfortunately, I was able to take off the weight sensibly, but was clueless about how to keep it off. That's when I began having bulimic episodes, where I would overeat, freak out, then force myself to vomit so I wouldn't gain weight. I kept myself thin for many years like this. It cost me my teeth, and my mental health. I was so ashamed of my behavior that it became my dark secret. It wasn't until much later in life that I was able to recover. One of my earlier recoveries led to me starting the first Overeaters Anonymous group for Anorexics and Bulimics in the Washington area. I thought of myself as the Bill Wilson of the vomit set. (Bill Wilson founded Alcoholics Anonymous.) While my recovery lasted less than a year, there were other women who went on to get healthy and stay healthy and free of their eating disorders.

My work at the clinic was going well. Everyone complimented me on my weight loss. I kept my technique for staying slim, that is my vomiting, well hidden.

Part of my counseling sessions were done with people who were on probation. I saw a few of these special clients on a regular basis, including one guy named Lenny. He was attractive but I don't think I ever really thought of him as anything more than a client. I did try very hard to let him know that I was his friend and that I would try to support him as best I could and he seemed to appreciate it.

All my counseling sessions went fine. I felt inspired and tried my hardest to come away from each session analyzing the interview and looking for areas where I could improve. As much as I enjoyed the work, the clinic was still a big strain on me.

The office politics bothered me terribly. When I first came in, it seemed that Thomas Drummond really approved of me. He made it well known how much he thought of me and how I improved as a counselor on an almost daily basis. Marsha was a social worker that worked at the clinic. It seems that when she first came Thomas and she got on well, and worked a great deal together. It was an uncomfortable situation because I was now taking up most of Thomas' time and that did not go down well with Marsha. It seemed she wanted to be the star and dominate Thomas' time. To that end I believe there were quite a few people she tried to manipulate and turn against me. It wasn't anything serious but it wasn't unusual for them to throw teasing remarks in my direction or have one of them roll their eyes at me after I'd spoken in a meeting. I really felt like they were ganging up on me and it hurt.

On Friday afternoons we closed the clinic early and around 3 o'clock it was party time. It was especially important for us to unwind and bond together by sharing stories about the working week and generally having a laugh. We usually had something alcoholic to drink, a few bottles of wine or a six-pack of beer. We sat around and talked, enjoyed each other's company, goofed about for a few hours and then left. One Friday I decided that we should have the party over at my dad's apartment, where I lived, just for the sake of a change. We drove over there, collecting a few bottles of wine on the way. I knew Dad would be out for at least a few hours so we decided to include a little music. We were playing drums and I showed Thomas my little wooden soprano recorder, which he made a good attempt at playing. Everything was going fine. Then I decided that would be a good idea if we had some marijuana brownies. I got some pot from Stuart. I didn't think anything of it because I sincerely believed marijuana wasn't in the same league as methadone, heroin and the other harder, more addictive drugs. We didn't say anything to Thomas about the brownies at first, we just invited him to help himself. Thomas had at least three brownies. I helped myself to a couple and another counselor, Heather, filled both hands with them cramming as many into her mouth as she possibly could. We all got pretty ripped, singing and dancing until it was time to leave. I wanted them to leave before my dad got home about eight o'clock that night and they were all out the door just in time. I don't know how they were able to drive because they were all very stoned but everyone made it home safely. That was absolutely the best clinic party we ever had.

As much as I loved that job I did manage to shoot myself in the foot once again.

Around noon one day I got a call from Lenny. He sounded upset and repeatedly threatened to violate his probation. I told him that would be entirely stupid as it would mean he was going to jail. He swore that if I didn't come over and talk to him he was going to do something stupid. I told him that I couldn't come over as he was on probation. The only place I could see him was in the clinic.

The phone line went silent before Lenny whispered. 'You don't come over and you'll regret it for the rest of your life.'

I panicked and told him to stay where he was and I'd be right over. I honestly thought I was doing a good deed.

I got to the address he had given me, which was a real rundown apartment in a crummy part of town. I went to the door, knocked, and when he answered he quickly ushered me in. I asked him what the matter was but all he wanted to do was hold on to me and tell me how good I looked. He asked me to sit down on the couch and kept leaning into me and pulling me into his personal space. I wanted to reciprocate his affection, I really did, but I resisted. I was flattered but I was there to try and keep him from hurting himself. At one point he pulled me close into his body, wrapped his arms around me and tried to kiss me.

'No Lenny,' I said. 'That is wrong, it would be entirely unprofessional of me.'

I told him he really needed to get over it and yet I felt so attracted to him and so wanted to kiss him back. I realized at that point that the only thing I could do was to pull myself out of there. I left when I realized everything was going wrong. Lenny wasn't happy, shouting all sorts of things after me but I was reasonably certain that he would be okay. He'd threatened suicide but I knew suicide personally and he was nowhere near that state of mind.

The next day Lenny called me and said that he really needed to see me. I told him that I could not see him other than our regular scheduled time at the clinic. He seemed a lot calmer and said if he came off probation then he could see me outside of the office. I agreed. I told him I would get him discharged from my caseload so that we could see each other outside of the office on a social basis. Was I a sucker.

The next opportunity I had to talk to Thomas about Lenny, I suggested that he was ready to come off probation. I expressed that we had done as much as we could for him and that he shouldn't have to come back to the clinic for counseling sessions anymore. Thomas agreed and Lenny was released from probation within a week.

A week later Thomas summoned me into his office. He closed the door and told me to sit down. He had a very stern look on his face. I didn't say anything, and at that point, although I knew something was up I honestly didn't know what the problem was. He looked at me, and said,

'Do you have something to tell me?'

'I don't think I know what you're talking about?'

'Jan, did you go over to meet with Lenny the other night?'

I couldn't believe it. How did he know that I went over to see Lenny?

'Well actually I did.' I was really caught completely off guard.

'And you know that's against the rules because he's on probation?'

'Yes,' I stammered. 'But it was an emergency.'

'There's no excuse, you know how wrong that is.'

I decided that I would tell the whole truth because I really didn't feel that I had done anything wrong. I knew the rules but occasionally they had to be broken or stretched a little at least.

'Lenny called me up, yes, and he was threatening to do something stupid. I went over there to try and help him. Under the circumstances I put his safety before the rules.'

Thomas was shaking his head.

'That's all there is to tell. Perhaps I should have mentioned it to you, but as nothing really happened I thought I would leave it.'

Thomas' look was very stern, he shook his head and then asked me to leave the office. I knew I was in trouble.

'You would have done the same Thomas.'

He looked up from his desk as I stood. 'No Jan, I wouldn't.'

The next few days were very tense. I sensed I was on the verge of being fired. I asked Thomas outright but he refused to answer me, saying he had to consult with some other people as he had a duty to report the incident.

I decided to beat him to the punch.

The next day I announced I would be leaving the office to get married. I caught everyone by surprise, including the poor guy I proposed to.

18

I was twenty-five in 1975 when I met Robert in a local bar. He was not terribly attractive but he was so obviously smitten with me that he smothered me with attention and that felt good.

He begged me to go out with him but I flatly refused. However, when I got back home the more I thought about it the more it seemed like a good idea, so I called him up a few days later. 'Bob, it's Jan. Please could you come over tonight as I really need some company?'

He couldn't get off the phone fast enough. 'Sure, I'll be there in half an hour.'

When Bob arrived that night, I had it all figured out. 'Will you marry me?'

I knew getting married would fix the situation in my office. Also, I was twenty-five years old and paranoid that I was over the hill. Bob was a decent guy and this way I could quit the office and save face. I wouldn't have to worry about supporting myself without a job.

I had been dating Tommy Armstrong, a counselor from the boys' division of the home. I really liked him a lot. The sex was the glue that seemed to keep the relationship together. I don't think Tommy had ever had a girlfriend as sexual as me but he wasn't about to jump headlong into marriage with me.

Bob, however, couldn't believe his luck. I knew I was the girl of his dreams because he kept telling me that every five minutes. He agreed to get married immediately. Looking back and reading this, you could be forgiven for thinking that it couldn't have happened like that, but I swear it did. There was absolutely no courtship, I had made up my mind and Bob was more than happy to go along with it.

Within a week I had an almost two carat diamond ring and the first task I had was to go to Tommy's apartment. It was only right to tell him face to face. Tommy was a little shocked at first but didn't put up any resistance. I even showed him the ring, which he approved of. He thought I was being foolish but wished me all the best and we parted as friends.

I started to plan what my dad would call 'The Big Party'. This was my $10,000 wedding. This was 1975, so in today's money that would be almost $48,000.

Getting ready for my wedding was overwhelming as I had no help. My father paid for it but I had to orchestrate everything. I arranged huge flower displays and the best catering my dad could afford and every imaginable facet of a big gorgeous Jewish wedding. I really wanted this wedding to be the best. Bob converted to Judaism. That gave me a measure of how committed he was to me and I was feeling good about everything. Surely, it would work out well, I thought to myself, but as the arrangements continued I sometimes wondered what the hell I was doing.

I purchased my gown at Claire Dratch, a very expensive boutique in Bethesda, Maryland. It really was a gorgeous gown and I did everything to look the part of the bride. It never dawned on me at the time that not only did I not love my husband but I was starting to develop a great deal of contempt for him. I'm honestly not sure why, but it was getting sour. This marriage was destined to end in disaster from the outset. I believe I resented him because he made me feel as if I needed him. More and more but I felt I didn't want him.

I was so confused. Mostly I was getting married because I thought I was supposed to. A big piece of my reasoning stemmed from the idea that I was getting old at twenty-five and would soon be considered over the hill. Plus, I had the mess at work! It just seemed like this would solve my situation. I never thought about love. I kept trying to play the part of the prospective bride but in reality I was just a little lost girl. I was not intimate with my husband at all because I wasn't sexually very attracted to him. We slept together once before the wedding during a drunken moment but it was an altogether forgettable experience.

The wedding arrangements hadn't exactly gone smoothly. Pulling everything together for the big day had been a nightmare as I'd managed it all on my own with no help from my mother. Ultimately it all came together and everything looked gorgeous. What a production. I had five bridesmaids, a maid of honor, and a ring bearer. Bob had his best man. The chuppah, the ceremonial canopy that hung over us, was magnificent. The rabbi had us sign the Ketubah and everything would have been perfect except for the fact that it was all a complete sham. I had absolutely no love for this man. I was lost.

Almost immediately there was an omen. My bridal bouquet disappeared just after the ceremony, never to be found. I had it as I walked down the aisle but then it went missing. I was terribly upset by this but knew that I just needed to keep going and get this whole thing over with. My parents, family and friends looked on proudly as the ceremony proceeded. Everything was traditional except for the fact that I was not in love with my husband. The entire event was a blur. I barely ate anything. I think I danced a little bit but I remembered almost nothing about being there as I was absolutely exhausted by the stress. Something closed in my brain that day, as if my inner self was trying to shut the whole thing off. It was just this thing that happened and the next thing and the next, and kisses and best wishes and hugs and congratulations and before I knew it Bob and I were married and leaving for our honeymoon.

Bob had arranged the honeymoon. He wanted to ski so we flew to Mont-Sainte-Anne in Quebec, Canada. We arrived at a tiny little chalet in a hotel complex, with nothing to do but ski. It was not my idea of a honeymoon but given the circumstances I could hardly complain. When we arrived at the hotel I was so exhausted that all I wanted to do was sleep. Bob had that honeymoon look on his face but I told him I was far too exhausted to think about anything like that. The reality was that I couldn't bear the thought of having sex with him.

The very next day we started our ski lessons. We spent all day on the slopes and that night we went to the bar where there was a one-man band. It was quite pleasant with a slightly older guy who sang mostly Billy Joel songs, particularly *Piano Man*, which he sang several times. When he sang *Piano Man*, he kept looking right in my direction. It was so obvious as he sang the lyrics. How did Bob not notice? This man was clearly trying making eyes at me.

At that point I had no sexual desire for my husband and wasn't sure what I was going to do when nighttime arrived. I decided to hit the champagne. When we got to the room I told Bob I was too drunk, rolled over and went to sleep. The next day we went out on the slopes by ourselves, Bob figured we'd learned more than enough in ski school the previous day. I had a problem with one of my skis constantly falling off so I kept tightening up the binding as I skied. Sure enough, I went over three moguls, small bumps, in the snow. The first two moguls I did very well but at the third one I got scared as I approached. The key to getting over these bumps is to relax, as I was able to do with the first two. No such luck for the third bump. I freaked out in mid-air, tightened up, tumbled over and landed with my legs sticking straight up in the air. Unfortunately, I had tightened my binding up so much it did not release and the ski spun like a helicopter, ripping all the ligaments in my left knee. I knew immediately that I had done some serious damage and could only lie in the snow, screaming in pain. The ski patrol was summoned and I was taken to hospital. X-rays determined I had broken no bones, but that the ligaments in my knee were torn badly. They put me in a removable splint and gave me no painkillers. I don't know what those doctors were thinking of because the pain was excruciating. Bob put me in a taxi to take me back to the hotel. It proved to be a major operation just to find the least painful way to get me in the back seat. I felt every bump and pothole in the road. We got back to the hotel and all I wanted to do was drink to obliterate the pain. Bob was very sympathetic and didn't push me to have sex. Eventually we went to bed. Bob didn't come near me that night. A good idea given the circumstances; sex was the last thing on my mind.

Bob had fallen in love with skiing and wanted to continue his time on the slopes. He spent all day skiing while I only had some magazines to keep me company. This hotel was not equipped with any way to amuse non-skiing clients. The bar and magazines were the only things the hotel offered to pass the time.

By the end of the morning, I was completely bored. My husband was out on the slopes and I decided what I really wanted to do was to go shopping. I called a taxicab company and a gorgeous young man came up to my room to pick me up. And that was exactly what he did because he put his big strong arms around me and carried me to his car. Suddenly my libido picked up a little and I began to experience a longing for sex, only not with my husband. My driver took me to a shop and picked me up again since I couldn't fend for myself. More importantly, I was getting a huge kick out of this Canadian hunk. I looked around the shop a little and asked him to pick me up to go back to the cab. As I settled into the back seat he looked at me and asked me where I would like to go next.

'To your house.'

He grinned. 'Certainly, madam,' and that's exactly what he did. When we arrived, he carried me over the threshold of his modest apartment and straight upstairs to his bedroom. We had an incredible afternoon of beautiful lovemaking. As dinner time drew close I knew my husband would be coming off the slopes and I decided it was time to go back to the hotel. I was feeling pretty wicked but was still in a bit of pain. I still couldn't believe those damn doctors hadn't given me anything so I decided that I would have to be my own doctor. When we got to the hotel I made a beeline for the bar and downed two Golden Cadillacs. They tasted more like a milkshake than booze, but as I never developed a taste for alcohol, they worked perfectly for me. I had my big strong taxi guy leave me on the bar stool. He told me that even with my splint on I looked beautiful. I kissed him gently on the cheek and told him we would meet up soon. He gave me his private number and went off to pick up some fares.

The piano player was there, making music and singing. Since I was alone he came over to me as soon as he finished his set. He started flirting with me straight away and I flirted back. He told me within five minutes that he wanted to make love to me. I explained to him that I was there with my husband but that we could easily figure out how to get together during the day when Bob was skiing. I gave him my room number and explained that my husband normally left for the slopes after eight. It wasn't long before Bob came into the bar. He had a great day on the slopes, and he absolutely glowed from his time skiing. I introduced him to the piano man, who quickly left. 'It was nice meeting you Jan,' he said. 'I'm glad you like my music.' He gave me a little wink as he walked away.

I shared another drink or two with Bob. He got me something to eat then carried me upstairs and put me to bed.

The next day Bob asked if I wanted to do anything in town.

'Don't be silly,' I said. 'Enjoy yourself skiing, I'll be fine. I'm sure I'll find something to amuse myself.'

Bob couldn't wait to hit the slopes, and was out the door early.

Sure enough, the piano man came knocking at my door soon after Bob had gone. I suspect he sat at the bar waiting for Bob to leave. I answered the door in the beautiful white negligee I had purchased as part of my trousseau. Piano Man immediately jumped on me, threw my crutches on the floor and lifted me onto the bed. We had an incredible couple of hours making love and then he left. I was exhausted but enjoyed every delicious second. I had a little lunch at the bar and then I was ready for some more action so I called the taxi man. He came by the hotel, picked me up and took me to his home. After many hours of lovemaking, he brought me back to the hotel and delivered me to my husband who was waiting for me at the bar. I told him I had been shopping and sincerely believe he didn't suspect a thing, even though I hadn't purchased anything.

The irony of the situation really hit me; the new bride had fucked everybody but her husband. I really didn't care and it bothered me that I didn't care. That night when Bob and I were at the bar having drinks, Piano Man kept winking and smiling at me knowingly. It was clear to me that my honeymoon was a preview of coming attractions.

When we got back to the U.S., I still hadn't officially consummated the marriage with my husband. I just couldn't bring myself to do it and blamed the pain in my knee, which was kind of half true because I was still in some discomfort. Fortunately, I immediately saw a doctor who gave me some great painkillers. I knew I had to eventually sleep with my husband. The strong pills helped me to put up with my husband in bed. Staying stoned on painkillers helped my marriage a great deal at that time.

We had been married for a few months when I decided that what I really needed to look good, was breast implants. Unsurprisingly. Bob thought it was a great idea because I told him if I felt good about myself it would lead to a greater, more fulfilling sexual relationship. I remember the plastic surgeon who was nicknamed the G!d, that was suggested to me by Hilda, the bartender at the Shoreham Americana, and I went ahead with it.

The job he did on my breasts was fantastic. No wonder he acquired such a glorious nickname.

Sexually, things didn't improve after my breast operation, at least not for my husband. As it turned out, he was not very secure in his own sexuality. I wondered if I had somehow sensed that all along and that was what put me off. I had no issues sexually, only with my husband. He kept hinting that he thought that there was something going on with me and other guys but never came right out and accused me of being unfaithful. What marked a real turning point were his disclosures about his sexual experiences. We talked about our sexual exploits quite often and one day he disclosed that he had once tried to have sex with a drag queen. At first he said it had only happened once. Then he said a couple of times and then it changed to 'every time I was with a drag queen', meaning he had been with queens quite a bit. He confessed that he loved the way they raved about his big cock, and loved Veda getting fucked in the rear by them or with a dildo. That completely turned me off him. What little sex we were having, stopped completely. Whatever obligation I felt to have sex with him vanished. I kept having plenty of sex but just not with him. I insisted that we have a sexually open relationship, and he agreed. Ostensibly he thought I was just giving him permission to have sex with drag queens. I was actually making sure any future sex I had with other men would not have to be hidden.

Things changed quickly. I'll never forget the time he came home when I was having sex with my neighbor and he offered to make the guy a sandwich. I'm not joking. I was on top of my neighbor, Paul, completely naked riding him like a jockey, when Bob walked in. My poor neighbor was mortified, blurting out his apologies as he struggled to pull on his trousers. Bob walked out of the room and I told my lover to relax.

Bob took a few minutes before he returned with a plate with some sandwiches. 'Would you like a sandwich Paul? Peanut butter and jelly?'

Paul didn't know what to do. 'Er...no thanks Bob.' He stammered, finished getting dressed and left.

The whole thing was just crazy.

Generally, I just hung around our apartment all day, as I wasn't working. I didn't need to. Bob had a great job as a cable man for the telephone company and supported us both. Mostly, I was bored. The only way I had to fill my days when my husband was at work was to have sex, go out shopping, get high or stay home and eat. Of course, whatever I ate was fattening, like pastries from the store in the shopping arcade below where we lived. And of course, whatever I ate I just threw up, as I would rather be dead than fat again.

My typical day would start with a little breakfast and then Bob would go to work. At around 11 or 12 o'clock I'd go shopping for some food on the ground floor. I would go into the little grocery store and buy at least four to five pastries, maybe a pint of ice cream and some things to make sandwiches, like bread and cheese and meat. I would return home and watch television and slowly stuff my face with the pastries and ice cream until I felt like I would pop. I would throw up, and then lie down and take a nap. When I woke up I'd start on the sandwiches, stuff my face, throw up and then sleep for a while. At about three or four o'clock I'd force myself from the sofa and spend the rest of my time getting dressed and primping so I would look nice for when Bob came home. It was a complete farce as by that time we weren't intimate at all. When he came home I would find excuses to get out of the house. I'd find a bar, eat and drink some more, but more often than not I'd spend the rest of the evening fucking my latest lover.

I had one memorable dalliance that lasted for quite a while with a man who lived in the same apartment building, on the level above us. He was a jeweler named Bert who was extremely talented and a really funny guy. When I went over to his apartment, Bert would play the most incredible soundtracks that were orchestrated so that by the time we got to the sex, the music and the rhythm of our bodies were in perfect sync. What came over his speakers can be best described as merry-go-round music, perfect for pumping up and down. What a crazy situation. I'd leave our apartment while Bob watched TV. Usually I told him I was going for a little shopping. Then I would pop upstairs for a passionate session with Bert. I'd come back after an hour or so hot and sweaty, with no shopping. How did Bob not suspect something else was happening? I guess he just stopped caring, though, if that was it, he never was direct with his concerns.

My drug abuse was not very extensive. I spent almost the entire year of my marriage getting high on pot and having sex with a string of lovers.

I knew this situation wasn't sustainable. I don't know how we finally figured out we'd be better off apart, but that day came. I really didn't love him. I didn't really hate him either. He was an okay guy, hardworking and kind. I just didn't love him and this farce was getting old.

So, after a year we concluded we had nothing in common and we decided to get a divorce. It was all very amicable, no arguments no fights, nothing. I was a little shaky about how I would support myself but I went back to live with my father, knowing I would figure it out from there.

I really didn't want to try another counseling job. The hours were long and the pay was horrible. I'd heard that you could make $35 a night plus tips working as a topless dancer so I decided to give it a try. I went to a bar called Shepard Park, which was a block from where I stopped the night I was raped. It was located on Georgia Avenue, near the dividing line between Washington and Maryland. Thirty-five dollars plus tips was not great, but it was better than what I made as a waitress. Besides, I was happy to show off my new breasts. I was a little worried because Shepard Park was a rough establishment but I knew a lot of the bikers that hung out there, so I decided to give dancing there a shot.

I had to audition for the owner and I could not believe that fate would be so cruel.

The man I had to dance for turned out to be Benim, the one who broke my heart in college. It was terrible seeing him again. I felt ill. My first instinct was to turn around and run. This was so strange but I gritted my teeth, went on a stage and danced a little routine. It lasted no more than three minutes and I got the job. Ben never spoke to me. He just watched my performance and then left. It was his manager who told me I got the job.

When it was time to start I just came and did my sets. Within a few weeks I had built up a nice stash of money, the $35 per hour plus the tips meant I could earn up to $100 on a good day, so once again I turned my attention to getting seriously high. I found a new guy who sold me heroin and I started going there more and more. His name was Ping Pong. He was an older black man, probably in his mid-fifties. He had good dope and the spoon, the unit measure, was good sized.

I'd go to Washington and look for Ping Pong as he would hang at a few different places. All I needed was $100 and it was enough for three or four decent hits. I kept it in a small folded piece of tinfoil. I would buy it and take it home. I kept syringes in my room but I never worried that my father would ever invade my privacy. I got pretty sloppy about leaving syringes out and even cluttered my room with bloody glasses of water that I used to wash out syringes. I was so depressed that I really didn't care about anything else other than getting high. My bulimia was getting terrible. I would go out and buy food and spend most of the day eating, then timed my vomiting to make my shift at the club. When I wasn't working, I hit the heroin. It was a pretty horrible existence

19

Things in my life were deteriorating. I was living at my dad's apartment and was basically just wasting time. I really didn't know what to do with myself. I was twenty-six years old and couldn't figure out what to do with my life. The only work I seemed to be able to do was dancing in sleazy bars. After Shepard Park, I worked for a gangster named Ernie. He was in his sixties and a really rough dude with a foul mouth. He came across like such a hick, without an ounce of sophistication. He was fat and bald, with a pushed-in face, always chomping on a hideous brown cigar. At first I just danced in his bars. He had three dancer bars, all in Washington D.C. One was in Georgetown; one was near Dupont Circle and the other was out in a really rough area of southeast Washington. Ernie kept showing up at work and talking to me. I think he sensed I had brains, which set me apart from most of the other dancers.

Finally, he asked me to manage the Georgetown bar which was great for me because it meant I wouldn't have to dance anymore. All that managing entailed was getting the girls in to work, serving beer, keeping tabs of the money and making sure that Ernie got the money at the end of the night. I never stole a penny from him and I think he knew it.

The Georgetown bar was pretty small. There was probably only room for about seventy patrons. Generally, I employed three girls a night, each doing twenty minutes sets. I was lucky that Georgetown was such a good location because it attracted some beautiful girls, which was really good for business.

I wasn't there very long when, sadly, one of my younger girls suddenly died. I later found out she had been abusing drugs extensively and that she finally overdosed. Her name was Wendy. Her mother asked me to attend the funeral so of course I went. Wendy had a lot of biker friends and the funeral procession included about forty bikes, mostly Harleys and Indians. The drivers were rough-looking dudes but they obviously thought the world of Wendy. It was heart-breaking when her mother spoke. She said goodbye to her daughter and kissed her on the cheek. She then announced that she was going to play her daughter's favorite song, *Dust in The Wind*, by Kansas.

Everyone was moved deeply. Even some of the tough bikers broke down, clearly distressed.

When I peered into the open casket and saw Wendy's beautiful face and her tiny twenty-two-year-old body, she only seemed to be asleep. It was hard to believe she was gone. Only a week ago she was dancing, drunk and bawdy, flirting with the customers on her platform high heels that pushed her height well above her tiny five feet, three inches frame. Her long and pin straight sandy-colored blonde hair flying everywhere as she undulated to the rhythms of the juke box.

The day seemed so surreal, her death, the funeral, the procession with the bikers...

When I got to work that night, I was feeling pretty somber. At one point I yelled for a moment of silence. I stopped the music and everybody thought I was crazy.

'Everybody lift your glasses,' I shouted out, 'and drink a last toast to Wendy's memory.'

We kept a minute's silence. Then the usual din resumed and Wendy was quickly forgotten.

I'd like to be writing now that Wendy's death affected me. That it made me look at my own drug addiction, because I'd witnessed a beautiful young girl in a coffin, and there was no doubt we were walking the same path. Unfortunately, nothing mattered. I completely blotted our similarities out of my mind. No lesson learned.

That evening when I finished my shift I'd be shooting up again.

Ernie told me I was doing a great job managing the place as it was becoming extremely popular. Customers were wall-to-wall. What I was particularly pleased about was the fact that we had quality customers. These were guys in suits and ties. I was meeting college professors and lawyers and pretty classy-looking clientele. I was proud of myself. On New Year's Eve the place was packed. We did more business that night than in the entire history of the place. Ernie was really proud of me too.

Just up the street from us was a bar called Good Guys. It was the same format as ours, beer and dancers. It was owned by my ex-boyfriend Ben. I always dreaded the thought that he would come walking into Ernie's bar, but he didn't. He stayed away.

There was a great story about the Good Guys and one of its dancers. Apparently Rod Stewart came in one night and swept one of their girls off her feet. I got the story from a bartender who worked there. He said the next day after Rod had been there, the manager got a call from a guy with an unmistakable British accent. No doubt it was Rod Stewart. He said the dancer would not be returning to work that night. Apparently he was quite taken with her. I never caught her name and I never did find out how long they lasted. All I could think of was why did Rod Stewart never walk into my bar? I did get to have a whirlwind romance with one of the local rockers though. He was a drummer, tall and lanky with long dark brown hair. Extremely sexy.

I always wore a real sexy teddy behind the bar when I served. Every now and then I would get coaxed to go up on the stage and dance and I had this one routine that always knocked everybody out. The William Tell overture would start and I would jump up on the stage and tap dance to it. Now, I never really studied tap dancing but I did a pretty good imitation of a Broadway showgirl. I even wore some high-heeled tap shoes, which made it sound that much more amazing. What a hoot.

One day the drummer came in after I had just finished my little dance. As I walked to the bar, he gently grabbed me by the wrist. 'I think I need to get to know you better.'

He looked deep into my eyes and I could feel myself being drawn into him. I ducked behind the bar and sat down on the little stool I had. He leaned across the bar and said, 'Get yourself a bottle of champagne.'

While it's true that most of the strip bars had a whole hustle around buying expensive bottles of champagne for the girls, we didn't have anything like that. We just served beer.

'Sorry,' I said. 'It's beer or nothing.'

He looked disappointed. 'I'll be right back,' he said, and disappeared out the front door. The night went on as usual, girl after girl, twenty minutes on, then the next. It was almost midnight when I felt a tap on my shoulder. I turned around and there he was with a huge bottle of Blanc de Blanc and two glasses. 'Can we sit down and do this?' he asked.

I looked into his gorgeous eyes. 'I should be working but I think I can pull this off if you really want to.'

'I do,' he said. 'I want it more than anything.'

I pointed across the room. 'That guy works as my busboy. He's called Randy and if he can cover for me it shouldn't be a problem.'

I knew before I even asked him that Randy would bend over backwards for me. Randy was forever grateful to me because I gave him a break when he really needed it. He came to work for me straight out of prison. When he approached me for a job he was honest about his circumstances and I appreciated that. I told him that I would hire him and give him a break. He wasn't even there a week when he asked if he could have an advance of $40 to buy some weed. I told him absolutely not. Later that night the till was short $40. What a coincidence.

I went to him and said, 'Randy, I know you took that $40. I'm going to put it back in the till and cover for you this time, but this time only. If there's ever so much as a nickel missing from this cash register you're out the door and out of a job forever.'

He was so eternally grateful that he became the hardest working employee in the establishment. Life is all about giving people a break. Randy covered for me and my drummer. We sat in a corner sipping champagne. When we began talking I was completely amazed. This guy was obviously educated and very articulate. He started talking about how this scene was so Kafkaesque. He brought Steppenwolf and the Theatre of the Absurd into the conversation. I was mesmerized but I had no problem keeping up with his intellect. We were both pretty taken with each other. He looked at me and said, 'I know it's a cliché, but what's a girl like you doing in a dump like this? This place is a dive and you don't belong here.'

I smiled. 'It's okay.'

I felt like Barbara Stanwyck in *Ten Cents a Dance*, all except the ending. She played a dancer in a sleazy dance joint in the thirties and in the end she marries a millionaire. I didn't think I was in any danger of anything like that happening to me, but I certainly could relate to feeling like a sleazy dancer.

He looked deep into my eyes again and said, 'I'm taking you home with me tonight. No questions, no objections, just tell me yes.'

I swooned under such seductive mastery. At closing time, he took me by the hand and never let go until we got into his apartment. We entered and he motioned me to sit on the edge of his bed. Then he cranked on some music and climbed into his drum set that was just off to the side. It wasn't massive but it was certainly large enough for an accomplished drummer to get a good workout. He told me to lean back and be comfortable, and I did. He played and played and I just let the music wash over me. It must've been one of the most complete seductions I've ever experienced. More than an hour later, when he was ready to make love to me, I was more than ready for him. We made love all night, with only a few breaks for him to get up and play the drums. We barely spoke a word. We didn't really need to. Our bodies did all the communicating that we needed.

To say that it was intense would be an understatement. Unfortunately, like all shooting stars, it burned out pretty quickly. The drummer dumped me a few weeks later. I was devastated. He dumped me because I was a little insecure girl and not the wicked dancer bitch he had seduced. He told me that I didn't act like a dancer. He wanted to move on. I felt heartbroken, and of course there were always drugs to console me.

About this time Ernie decided that he wanted me to manage his bar, called the Fireplace, near Dupont Circle. The set up at this joint was pretty similar, with one big difference; we served mixed cocktails. Most of the mixed drinks weren't that tough, you just measured a shot of booze and then filled it up with mixer. However, one day a gentleman ordered a Bloody Mary and I was at a complete loss as to what to do. I could only guess what went into it. I knew that the alcohol was vodka, so I threw a shot of vodka into a shaker and then threw in some ice. I knew there was tomato juice so I threw some of that in too. The rest was all guesswork. Tabasco sauce, Worcestershire sauce and salt was the best I could come up with. I shook it all up, poured it into a glass and served it with a smile. Fortunately, I was wearing an extremely low-cut teddy that night and made sure that I bent over when I talked to him. When he went he left me a $20 tip, which was remarkable because the drink was only five dollars. I figured I must've done a good job on making the drink. When I picked up his glass I noticed that he barely touched it. I decided to taste it. It was the most disgusting concoction imaginable. It was then that the picture became crystal clear. Sex sells. I never worried about my bartending skills again after that.

My heroin abuse had escalated. I was doing well at Ernie's, he paid me well and the tips were more than generous. That meant only one thing...more heroin and more highs. I was shooting so much dope I started having trouble finding a vein in the bend of my arm, so I started shooting in other places, mostly my wrists.

The heroin was easy to get a hold of at Ernie's. There was always someone in on the scene, though to the best of my knowledge Ernie was never a part of selling it and neither was anyone at the club. However, I'm sure there were plenty of drugs on the premises, even if I knew nothing about them.

A few Selective Service cops used to hang in the club and we were quite friendly with them. They were real cops and only guarded foreign embassies and eminent dignitaries, as opposed to patrolling the streets. At least that was my understanding. I went out a couple of times with one of them, named Sam. We would often head for breakfast in Chinatown after closing time, around 4 o'clock. One day after breakfast I remembered I'd left my purse back at the club and Sam offered to drive me back there.

As we walked in through the door of the club I noticed it had been forced open. Just then a big black dude walked towards us carrying a crate of booze. He didn't belong in my place of business at 5 o'clock.

'Sam!' I screamed. 'You're a cop, do something!'

It was late and Sam was tired, so it took him a while to respond. It seemed like forever before he reached for his gun. 'Police!' he yelled. 'Put your hands up and don't move.' Next thing I knew he was carting the guy away.

It was actually quite comical, and Sam never got tired of bringing up the incident. Of course, in Sam's version, he was a hero. When I told the story, he was more of a joke.

Not long after this happened, another man started paying serious attention to me. He was spending a lot of cash at my bar and afterwards took me out for champagne and lobster breakfasts. It appeared that money was plentiful as he was always throwing it in my direction.

I went out with him a couple of times until Sam pulled me aside. He told me this guy was an undercover customs agent looking to bust the club for supplying drugs to the patrons. I was furious. I'd been duped. This man wasn't interested in me.

It turned out that one of the dancers' boyfriends were busted for drugs, and to try and get leniency he offered up a story that we were a big-time drug-dealing place. He suggested I knew something about the drugs and the agent took it from there.

I was angry. I formulated a plan. I would play along with his little game and set up a scam. I would give him plenty of information about drugs, only none of it true. I stayed up late at night with him on the phone, spinning tales of drug importers, clandestine airfields where drugs were delivered, and more. I told him my dad was worried about the guys calling me with Columbian accents. I laid it on thick.

My next phase, I decided, was to figure out a way to have him take me to Beverly Hills and await a phony drug deal at the Wilshire Hotel.

I had it all planned. However, when I mentioned my little ruse to Sam he went crazy. 'You don't know these dudes, Jan. You can't mess with them.' He said if I went ahead with my scam, they'd plant drugs on me and then bust me. I couldn't take the chance it would backfire so I had to come up with something else. This guy wasn't going to play me.

I knew the perfect way to show him what a schmuck he was.

I managed to call his house when he was not there. He had given me his phone number, but did not do a good job of coaching his roommate. When the roommate answered, I told him I was a friend and wanted to speak to him at the Customs Office. He assumed I was cool, and did not hesitate to give me the number. I called immediately, and randomly got right through to him.

'Agent Riley', he answered.

'Hi guy! This is Jan. Just thought I'd call you at work.'

There was total silence. He knew his cover was blown.

So much for feeling like James Bond. I figured this was the safest way to end it all.

20

I needed money so I kept dancing at clubs. When I was in the club scene, I was walking a dangerous emotional tightrope. Because of the rape I was extremely upset about anyone coming on to me sexually. Drugs destroyed any sense of self-esteem or self-worth. I believe these two human traits are what keep women from exploiting their sexuality for money. (I'm talking about street prostitution and selling oneself through marriage.)

   I would think that a strong sense of one's self-worth is what keeps women above those means. I didn't have those gifts to keep me from selling myself out. The irony is that I believe it was the rape that kept me away from prostitution. It wasn't that I felt I was too precious. I was just so repulsed by the sexual aggression.

There was a period when I just felt too burnt out to dance. I was staying at my dad's apartment, so I didn't need a lot of money to survive. My dad figured out the bulimia, so he would give me $10 a day for food. It didn't leave me enough to get high, so for a short period of time, I had to stand my life straight. The only way I could afford my drugs was if I danced. So, it was only a matter of time before I returned to dancing.

It did not take long for me to become addicted to heroin. This was a dangerous place to be: I honestly did not care if I was dead or alive, so I got myself, and kept myself, as fucked up as possible.

Previously I had always been careful not to develop a physical addiction. I would take a break from the heroin, usually doing a lot of speed, and that system seemed to work.

Things changed radically. If I did not have a steady supply or if I tried to take a short break from smack, I got sick. The first sign was that my nose would start running. Then my backbone would start to hurt. If I waited too long, it would feel like I was getting stabbed in my spine.

I panicked. I could not handle these changes. I couldn't stand my life the way it was. Even though I might have been able to tough it out, I just felt completely lost and wanted someone else to take over.

I had to check myself into a hospital.

21

I went over to the emergency room at Montgomery General Hospital and told them that I needed help. I was addicted to heroin and I needed to detox.

They were happy to admit me to their short-term psychiatric ward. There they would gradually taper me off the narcotics I was addicted to. Or at least that was the theory. I had heard that my physician, Dr. Chambers, was very easy to get over on, so when asked how much heroin I was using, I lied my ass off. I exaggerated the amount I was doing by about four times. My first dose of detox knocked me on my ass. I was high as a kite and everybody knew it. Fortunately, Dr. Chambers didn't seem to care that I looked higher in my 'detox', than when I entered. He was a former addict, which was supposed to give him some special insight into addiction. Whatever his philosophy was, it was okay by me because he let me have as much dope as I wanted. I was happy. I spent the first forty-eight hours nodding, high as a kite. It made the time go fast and although the high on methadone was not as pleasurable as the high on heroin, it was good enough. Heroin gives you a nice warm feeling that leaves you feeling invincible. There is also a warm rush that is highly pleasurable. It makes you happy and mellow, like pure love and peace. Nothing bothers you, which is why it's called a troubled man's drug.

Mealtimes would've been embarrassing if I cared, but I didn't. I spent most of the time falling face first into plates of food. Despite the mess I was just happy to be high.

Finally, I admitted that I had probably miscalculated the amount of dope I was doing so they recalculated my dosage. I came back down to earth with a thud. It was a drag landing, mostly because where I landed was this boring hospital with very little to do to break the monotony of the day. After thirty days I was released, went back to live my father and back on heroin.

Every thirty-day stay was pretty much the same. Altogether there were at least thirty to forty short term hospital detoxes, and they all went pretty much the same.

Then I met Tiger.

He had wavy dark brown hair, very deep-set dark eyes and a great smile. He was kind of stocky and about my height. He had a funny way of talking that I could not describe in a million years, though he sounded more like he was talking at me, rather than to me. It was as if he felt he had to force me to pay attention to him. We had nothing to do but talk so we ended up telling each other the story of our lives. His was interesting. He shared how his dad had played with Tommy Dorsey's band, decided to quit the band and settled in Annapolis Maryland. He had enough money to buy a boatyard, which became extremely successful. Tiger's family had money, though Tiger didn't. They lived in a really nice house that was part of the boatyard and owned other properties in Annapolis as well.

Tiger and I bonded quickly and became inseparable. The fact was we really had nothing better to do and this was a great way to distract ourselves from our misery. We would sneak around and manage to find short moments of privacy in unguarded closets, where we would kiss and snuggle. It was exciting and combated the boredom. The hospital was surprisingly lax as far as security went. Tiger was very thoughtful about not pushing me sexually, which I appreciated since I needed to feel safe. With him I also felt desired and loved. He was kind and tender. He never made any judgment on anything I had to say. He was so accepting. I honestly felt like there was nothing I could say to him that would shock him. He was the first person I was ever able to talk to about my bulimia. Even though he didn't understand the condition he just accepted me for who I was. This was huge for me. I felt so much shame and humiliation and he just shrugged his shoulders as if to say, 'Big deal, who cares?'

After we became an item I actually started to enjoy my time in the hospital and awoke every morning happy to just be with him. I couldn't remember feeling that way for a long time. We were really good for each other and we loved being in each other's company. As for the therapeutic part of being there, well that was kind of incidental. The most important part of the experience for me was that I had found Tiger and he was my man.

When we went to the therapy groups, we tried to join in and participate because we knew we had to do all the activities if we wanted to get better. The truth was that we both wanted to get clean and live normal lives, we both knew how fucked up we truly were and felt terribly lost. But we talked about hope and prayed that with our new love we would find a better life and kick this terrible drug habit forever. The closer it came to our release date the more afraid we were. We knew that once we got out it was going to be tough to stay clean.

When it was time to leave we decided that we would live together. His family owned a house in Annapolis, just a block away from the boatyard, so we set up house there. Fortunately, when we first moved in we were able to stay busy, trying to make the house comfortable. It was completely furnished with nice, homely décor, nothing extravagant but it had a warm feel to it. I brought very little with me, basically the clothes I had at the hospital and a few things I picked up at my father's home that were meaningful to me. I brought the round black and white Japanese papier-mâché box that belonged to Lise, and a little hand-painted pale blue coffee mug with her name printed in dark blue on the side. She made that mug at camp when she was about ten, and both items were very precious to me. They were the only two objects I had left that had belonged to my sister and I cherished them dearly.

Neither Tiger nor I worked at that time. He had some money saved up so we were okay for food and gas for the car, but not much else. We really didn't have much to fill our days and that was our downfall. If only we had jobs we would have had something to focus on, something to keep our minds busy. The old adage about idleness being the devil's playground is certainly true.

One day I was lying around the house, not doing much, when Tiger rushed in and headed for the bedroom, closing the door between us.

'Hey,' I said. 'What are you up to?'

He didn't even open the door, just shouted. 'Nothing. Do you mind leaving me alone for a while? I have a headache and I'm feeling crummy.'

This was unusual. Even though we had only been together a short time, I knew his behavioral patterns. Whenever we had been apart and reunited, he would always give me a big hug and ask me how I was doing. He wouldn't hang any place else in the house except with me unless he had something specific to do.

Something was up. 'Do you mind if I come in and hang out with you? I'm really bored.'

'Come on Jan, I've got a headache,' he shouted. 'If you don't mind, I'd really like it if you would just leave me alone for a little while.'

I was crushed. I couldn't imagine why Tiger was blowing me off. How could he have become tired of me so quickly? I only wanted to lie on the bed with him. I got up and quietly walked over to the bedroom door. I turned the knob.

It was locked. I started pounding on the door. 'Hey Tiger, open up.' I could hear him fumbling around with something.

'Come on Jan, play the game and just leave me alone for little while.'

No way was I giving up. I banged and shouted for him to let me in. Finally, he opened the door. Sure enough, when I looked into his eyes I could see he was high. I was so disappointed. Everything we had worked for was destroyed at that moment. What was the point? All those weeks in the institute, all our promises to the staff, but worse…our promises to each other.

'You got high, didn't you?'

'Well, not really,' he slurred.

'What do you mean not really, Tiger? Your eyes are absolutely pinned and you look stoned.'

Finally, he admitted to it. 'It's true, I went to buy some dope but what I got was garbage. I was going to bring you some back but it was so bad I didn't bother.'

It didn't take for the sheer disappointment to turn into desire as the addict in me took over. 'Where did you go to score?'

'Just a guy I know who lives around the corner.'

'Well shit, no wonder. The dope is shit here. You have to go to Washington to get anything decent.'

He looked up at me through the tiny slits his eyes had now become. 'You know where to score good dope?'

'Of course I do. You have to go to D.C. to get good shit.'

He looked deep into my eyes and I melted. 'Let's go,' I said, and in the blink of an eye we were back in the throes of addiction. We were getting high again. Montgomery Hospital was ancient history. The time we spent plus the hopes and dreams and promise of a healthy future, all down the toilet in an instant. Going to D.C. to score dope was all that mattered at that moment.

Finding dope was easy. We waited until we were back home to get off.

As I pulled my belt tight around my bicep and prepared to shoot up I never gave the hospital another thought. I felt no guilt, had no thoughts for the doctors and therapists who had spent so much time with me. All I wanted to do was get high.

I was much more successful scoring heroin in Washington than Tiger was. From then on I would go down by myself to find dope. I'd use some of it to get high while I was there and bring home what was left. There really is no honor among junkies. Tiger knew he was getting shortchanged and insisted on going on his own again, thinking he could do better without me making the score disappear by half.

Big mistake. He got ripped off for all our dope money. He developed a new appreciation for my scoring skills. It wasn't long before all of this became way too depressing to deal with. I decided to go back into detox.

Tiger wanted no part of going back. I was severely bulimic and quite thin at this point. I don't think Tiger understood what made people want to throw up their last meal. When I was readmitted into the hospital for detox, I was physically quite ill. It wasn't determined exactly what was wrong with me and they put me in a medical bed.

Tiger and I decided that we should get married and we appealed to the doctor to let us get married in the hospital. You couldn't do anything without the doctor's permission, not even obtain a marriage certificate.

The doctor refused. He told me that he couldn't sanction a marriage of two drug addicts and that we would have to wait until we were clean. I was furious but deep down I knew he was right.

22

It was decided that it would be best to admit me into a treatment center called Hazelden, which was located in Center City, Minnesota. By this time, I had spent the majority of my adult life going in and out of institutions. It was like a revolving door that never seemed to stop. I hated my life. Even Tiger couldn't lift me out of the depression. I agreed to go to Hazelden because I felt there were no more options for me. My physician, Dr. Chambers, had been a patient there and he had total faith in their ability to help me recover.

I flew out to Hazelden in a mental fog that did not lift when I arrived. At the airport I was met by a driver with a sign that said 'Jan Kasmir'. He was friendly, helped me with my luggage and then we made the long drive to Center City.

I was admitted to the infirmary at Hazelden. They took all my luggage, which I guessed would be searched. I didn't bring anything I wasn't supposed to, so I didn't worry about it. This was it for me, I was really determined and serious about trying to do the right thing. I didn't want to go back to the streets, to dancing and constantly putting myself in harm's way. As I would later hear, I was sick and tired of being sick and tired.

At Hazelden there was none of Dr. Chamber's 'intox' special where he let me have as much methadone as I wanted. They were taking everything very seriously. I was honest about the amount of drugs I was doing, but when it was time to get my first dose of medicine it barely kept me from feeling sick. 'I honestly don't think I've had enough medication. I'm feeling pretty lousy,' I said to the nurse.

She listened attentively and then offered, 'I can retake your vital signs now and if there is a significant problem, we will absolutely address it.'

I nodded, convinced that something would show up and I'd get more methadone. Needless to say, there was nothing wrong with any of my vital signs. There was no high blood pressure, I didn't have a temperature and I actually looked pretty calm for somebody who was supposed to be in such dire straits. I was pronounced medically sound. She refused to give me any more medication.

I saw that things were going to be different this time and hoped it was a positive sign of things to come.

I was introduced to the other patients and could participate in various activities, like group therapy sessions, lectures and, of course, AA meetings. One of the first lectures I attended was led by an old-timer named Ben. He was a tiny guy, about five foot four, snow-white hair still peppered with some grey, and a grizzly long beard to match. He shared how he travelled around the Indian reservations going to various AA meetings. 'I attended a meeting at this reservation that was really way out in the wilds of Minnesota. They rarely got strangers to visit their reservation but I was happy to go. The meetings were conducted in the usual manner and I really enjoyed them and felt the guys got a lot out of what I had to say.'

He related how at the end of one meeting, an elder pulled him aside and shared that he had a concern that was very pressing and he wanted to ask Ben's opinion.

'The elder said that if one of their AA members got drunk, the way they would deal with it was to beat the hell out of them and drag them back to a meeting.'

Everyone in the room gave a collective groan, me included. This was not the way to treat an alcoholic.

We stayed silent as Ben continued. 'The elder wanted to know what I thought about this. He wanted to know if they were doing the right thing.' He paused for effect and then grinned. 'I told him to keep doing whatever worked.'

Everyone howled. We fell about laughing, even though we knew that the story was no joke.

Ben was a real character. I loved listening to his stories about AA and sobriety. Once he told me how Hazelden got its name. A bunch of sober and not so sober drunks would come to Hazel's farmhouse for AA meetings. They decided to call it 'Hazel's den', to honor her 12-steps work. The 12th step was where you repay your gift of sobriety by carrying the message to other suffering alcoholics. Hazelden became a place for drunks to recover.

Even though my problem was drugs, I learned that there really was no difference between using drugs and alcohol. I was addicted to the experience of intoxication. I was told to shut up about drugs and just identify with the core issues.

Our days were mostly spent in group therapy though there were many lectures we had to attend as well. There was so much to learn about addiction, and about the twelve steps of Alcoholics Anonymous. Hazelden's staff promised me that the twelve steps would work for me. While in treatment we had to work the first four steps of the program. To finally graduate we had to do a fifth step. It was all very confusing.

The first step was to admit that I was powerless over alcohol, or in my case drugs, and that my life had become unmanageable. It was explained to me that I was addicted to the experience of intoxication and it didn't really matter if it was drugs or alcohol, we all ended up in the same place.

'It doesn't matter if you take a bus or a train to New York, either way you end up in New York. Regardless of how you get high, your life becomes unmanageable.'

That made sense to me. I also had no argument with the idea that my life was unmanageable. In fact, it was a fucked-up mess.

So, I got it.

Now I was ready for the second step, which was to believe that a power greater than myself could restore me to sanity. The first assumption in this step was that I was insane. I wouldn't need restoring to sanity if I wasn't insane. I had no problem believing that I was insane. The part that was tricky was about a higher power and how it could restore me to sanity. I honestly knew that I believed in G!d, but at this point I could not believe that G!d believed in me, and even if he did, then why let me get so fucked up? I felt like such a complete failure that I couldn't believe that I was worthy of anyone's effort. Not even G!d should care about me. That's when everyone explained to me that I was making it way too complicated. I just had to believe that there was something greater than myself, something or someone that I could believe in. I was told that I could make anything I wanted to into my higher power. A table or a chair could be my higher power or the group could be my higher power. The important thing was that anything could be my higher power that wasn't me.

Okay, so I felt I got the second step. Step Three was extremely hard. I was told that I had to make a conscious effort to turn my will and my life over to the care of G!d as I understood him. First of all, I did not understand him and secondly it sounded like such a big deal. I had no idea how I was going to handle this. Whatever concept I had of G!d was so shaky that I wasn't sure what I could expect from him, and how to turn my will and my life over to him. It sounded complicated. What could that possibly mean?

I struggled but they persevered with me. They said all I had to do was make a decision. That was all…just make the decision and the rest would fall into place. I thought I could handle that.

Then it was time for me to face what they called 'the wreckage of my past.' In Step Four I had to make a searching and fearless moral inventory. I was supposed to be face my past unafraid. This was tough because I spent all my life fearful and I didn't know how I was suddenly supposed to become fearless.

And then, Step Five. I had to admit to G!d, myself and another person the exact nature of my wrongs. It was frightening and embarrassing. I could barely face myself; how could I face another person? I was worried that all was lost and I could not imagine how I was going to get through all of this.

I went into my shell and became withdrawn.

People consoled me with good advice. 'Remember it's a cinch by the inch, but hard by the yard', 'One day at a time' and 'You can eat an elephant one bite at a time'. All this advice was meant to help me not get overwhelmed by the daunting tasks ahead of me. 'It's a simple program for complicated people.'

I tried to do everything that I was told to do, but if I'm honest, I mostly just walked around in a fog. I felt lost and hopeless and still craved heroin, only there was no possibility of getting any here in the middle of nowhere. I did my best to hide my feelings but I suspected they knew I was lost. After all, they had seen thousands of cases like mine.

The thirty days that I was supposed to be there absolutely flew by and the next thing I knew I was writing a paper called, 'My fourth step', which was supposed to be the key to my being released. I finished my part; I made a searching and fearless moral inventory of myself, to the best of my ability, the day before it was due. I stayed up late writing down every horrible thing I could think of that I had done. I included where I felt I had gone wrong in my life. There was some nasty shit in there and I honestly didn't care how accurate it was. I just wanted to do it, get it over with and get out of there. I was trying but I was lost. I was lost and afraid of letting anybody know how lost I was.

The next step was to share this horrible information with my counselor. We sat in his office for something like three or four hours, while I spilled my guts. Even though I did not begin the session completely committed, I felt cleansed when the whole experience was over.

My counselor pronounced my effort as successful, and I was told I would be leaving in a day.

The next day there was a short graduation ceremony where those of us who had completed the fifth step were given recognition and a graduation medallion. Everyone wished us all the best on our journey into a clean life, and as abruptly as it started, it was over. Now it was time to face reality.

23

I returned to live with my dad, which was a mistake. Within a few weeks I went back to Tiger and Annapolis and, of course, relapse was right around the next corner, as Tiger was still getting high. I knew this was all a horrible mistake and I knew I had to get back to Hazelden as quickly as possible. I begged my dad to put me on a plane back to Minnesota and the next thing I knew I was back at Hazelden. It was truly a great relief.

They felt that the short-term program was just not enough time for me, and I entered their long-term treatment program. That was the same as the short-term program except slowed way down and it included working on the premise that one could manage some responsibility. I was told treatment could last up to eighteen months which seemed an awfully long time, and even that could be extended if they thought it was necessary. I can't explain the euphoria I experienced; I was so happy to be back in Hazelden where I felt safe. I truly felt safe. I honestly felt that these people understood my problem and could help me.

Unfortunately, they didn't really know how to address my bulimia. I opened to them and shared the fact that I was eating and vomiting up my food several times a day. In fact, at this point it was extremely hard for me to keep any food down. I was still so petrified of getting fat. I continued to be plagued by my bulimia and sneaked around, hiding my condition, vomiting up food in the toilets, making sure there was no one around to hear me. I was starting to feel isolated and lonely. In my eyes my bulimia branded me as a terrible person.

I made friends with an eighteen-year-old boy named Jan. We loved the fact that we shared the same name and thought that meeting was our destiny. I was twenty-eight at the time. He was over six feet tall, and weighed close to three-hundred pounds. He had a sweet, open face, with relatively short, thick and curly sandy-colored hair. One day we decided that it would be beneficial for us to share our worst secret with each other. I was going to tell him an aspect of my life that made me the most ashamed and he was going to do the same. We would pick a secret that we'd never been able to tell anyone else. At Hazelden I had only shared my bulimia with my counselor and a few of my group therapy members so it was a big deal to me. My humiliation was so deep and I found it very painful to open to other people.

I shared first. 'This is really hard for me to talk about. It's something that I've never been able to share with practically anyone. It even makes me feel ill right now, just the thought of talking about it.'

'I'm here for you,' Jan said. 'Whatever it is, I promise you that I'll still care about you.'

'Honestly? I need to know that if I'm gonna be able to get the words out of my mouth.'

'Come on, you can do it,' he said. 'You know they say you're only as sick as your secrets. Don't hold onto it, you'll feel really better if you share it.'

I took a deep breath. 'Okay, here goes. After I eat I throw up what I've eaten because I'm afraid I'll get fat.'

He sat back in his seat while a puzzled look played across his face.

'Are you kidding me Jan? Is that it? I thought that you were going to tell me you had murdered somebody.' He started to laugh, shaking his head.

'I am so sorry that it makes you feel bad Jan, because quite honestly I don't think it's a big deal.'

I was incredulous. It was not the reaction I had expected. 'Okay Jan, now it's your turn. What's your biggest secret?'

He started to go bright red in the face. Clearly, he didn't want to tell me his secret.

'Come on Jan, I did it. I shared my deepest secret. I feel better now. Come on, give it a shot. What do you have bottled up inside of you? What's your big secret?'

It seemed like he hung back forever. He was having a terrible time opening his mouth and getting out his big secret. Finally, he blurted out, 'I'm a virgin.'

I couldn't believe it. That was the big secret? I sat there for a moment while he squirmed, looking me in the eyes then quickly diverting his look. Then I shook my head. 'Jan, I don't know how to break this to you.'

He looked up from the floor.

'But that really isn't a big deal. You're still only a teenager and that's fine. Maybe you're saving yourself for somebody special. I don't even understand how that could make you feel bad. Everybody here loves you! I promise you that nobody would think anything bad about that.'

We both started laughing. Each of us had held onto the secret that we thought was absolutely the most horrible for any human being. What a relief it was to get these secrets out. We both felt that a hundred-pound boulder had been lifted off our chests. We laughed about it the whole day.

Shortly afterwards Jan was transferred to a facility for teenagers with addiction problems. He had been addicted to pills. I was so sad to see my dear friend go but we promised to meet up again once we were both clean.

Dorothy was my main counselor. She always had a warm smile on her face. She called me into the office one day saying she had something important to tell me. I walked in and took a seat as she squeezed in behind her desk. I'll never forget the pained look on her face.

'What is it?'

'It's Jan.'

My face lit up. 'He's here? Can I see him?'

'No Jan, sorry. I knew you two were so close.'

As I looked at her sad expression I knew something was up.

'I'm sorry.'

'What? What is it, tell me?'

'He died last night. He committed suicide by hanging himself.'

I was shocked. Stunned. Dorothy's words broke my heart. I could not stop crying. Jan was such a sweet being, and only eighteen years old.

This all transpired during the third month of my stay at Hazelden. I could not cope with the pain of Jan's death. I buried my feelings by not talking about how upset I was. I have come to understand a strange metaphor that is played out with bulimia. Instead of dealing with my pain by crying, I stored up my hurt by not allowing myself to express my grief. At some point those buckets of tears were too much to hold onto, and I metaphorically purged the tears by throwing up my food. I literally threw up my tears instead of shedding them.

It took a month for me to explode. I was just about to complete my fourth month when I got into trouble. We all went to a local country fair. I got hungry, left the group and walked over to check out the food concessions. I immediately lost control and proceeded to stuff my face with an incredible array of junk food: hot dogs, cotton candy, ice cream, bread pretzels, waffles. You name it, I ate it, until I was so stuffed I could hardly move. I then had to find a secluded place where I could throw up all the stuff I had consumed. There was no way I could let that stay in my stomach too long as it meant I would have gained at least five pounds. Easily. I was so hung up in the drama with this binge, I didn't realize that our departure time came and went. We were supposed to all gather at a certain point at 5 o'clock but I was so busy gorging myself that I completely lost track of the time. It was after 6 o'clock when I resurfaced at the original meeting place. Everybody was fuming. I knew I was in trouble. When we got back to Hazelden, I had to report to the counselors' office to speak with Dorothy. I felt sheepish about the whole thing. Mostly they just want to make sure they got to the bottom of everything that happened.

Dorothy said. 'So you want to tell me what you were doing? You know everybody waited over an hour for you until you showed up. They were really worried. What were you up to?'

I felt like a naughty schoolgirl. 'I'm really, really sorry Dorothy. I just couldn't help myself. I really had to eat; I was starving.' I don't think she believed me.

'That was completely selfish and irresponsible,' she said. 'We were very worried about you; we didn't know what had happened to you. You showed no consideration for the group.'

Dorothy was mad and I didn't realize how serious the trouble I found myself in, was. She put me on probation. 'If you screw up anything, and I mean if you have one vomiting episode, you are out of here!'

I had no idea how I was going to adhere to this. I had tried to stop so many times without any success. I knew I was being set up to fail, but I had no way to protest. 'Dorothy, there is no way that I can promise I'll stop. I really try but it just takes hold of me.'

'It has to stop Jan. If you want to stay here, you'd better figure out how to do it. End of discussion.'

I was terrified. I didn't know what I was going to be able to do differently. Sure enough, within the week I had an episode where I voluntarily vomited. I made an appointment with Dorothy and confessed. I needed help with this as much as I needed help with my drug addiction.

It didn't make any difference to Dorothy that I turned myself in. I thought I would be safe but I was kicked out and told to leave the following day.

I was broken-hearted. A driver took me and my luggage to Minneapolis, and my dad arranged for me to check into a hotel in downtown Minneapolis.

24

The following morning, I telephoned one of the counselors I had seen in addition to Dorothy, and brought him up to date with my expulsion. He was off for a few days while this all took place and had no idea about the details of my expulsion. He said he was horrified and would be right over to see what he could do. When he arrived, I opened the door and he immediately grabbed my hand and started to kiss me. I was shocked but as usual I responded. He was nice enough. He wanted me and that felt good. He took me to bed and fucked the hell out of me.

I was not exactly expecting this kind of visit. I was always up for sex but this caught me by surprise. I knew it was completely inappropriate, but apparently he hadn't figured that out. Anyway, when it was over, he consoled me with a hug and then left.

I still had faith in Hazelden despite my failure, so I called Dorothy and begged her to let me come back. After about fifteen minutes of pleading she reluctantly agreed but warned me there would be no more chances.

I checked out of the hotel, took a taxi and was sitting in her office within an hour.

I had to get through the next thirty days with no incidents. I knew it wasn't enough to pretend I was going along. No matter what happened, I had to follow the rules, because I knew I would rat myself out if I faltered.

A few days after I returned, I was lying in bed, thinking. And I started having a conversation with G!d that would forever change my life. I appreciate that it is difficult to believe me when I say that I spoke with G!d, but I have no doubt that I did, and the fact that I can look back over forty years and see my reprieve from a life of addiction, proves me out.

I was very shaky about whether or not I could get clean, and stay clean. I looked up towards the heavens, and said out loud, 'G!d, I promise you if you let me get clean this time, I will do something specifically for women. I promise to repay this gift by doing something to help alcoholic women.'

Almost immediately I fell into a deep sleep, which was unusual because often I'd lay awake for hours, staring at the ceiling. When I woke up the next morning, the first thing I thought about was keeping my promise to G!d by helping alcoholic women.

The program at Hazelden lasted thirty days. The only sad result was that I knew I had to keep Tiger out of my life. I was determined to stay clean. Tiger wasn't. It was simple. If I stayed with Tiger I would be back on heroin. It was inevitable.

I needed to get away from him and our old haunts where we had easy access to dealers and dope. I committed to one more thirty-day stay at Hazelden, which transpired uneventfully. When I graduated my final time from the program, I made a conscious decision to move somewhere where I knew nobody. Some place where I could make a fresh start.

I chose to stay in Minneapolis. It was over a thousand miles away from Tiger. It seemed as good a place as any to start a new life. My dad agreed to pay for an apartment I found that was $400 a month. It was just across from Loring Park, which was just a few blocks from the old Guthrie theatre. I later found out that I moved across from a big gay pick-up spot. It seems that young gay boys would stand around anywhere on these three blocks and look hot. All night long, beautiful cars would cruise up and down the block with men trolling for their next boyfriend. It wasn't really dangerous; it was just a little concerning. It started to make me wonder how prolific the heterosexual population in Minneapolis was. It did turn out that heterosexual women had a hard time finding dates. In fact, the ratio of men to women was so weighted against women that absolutely fabulous, well-educated and beautiful women were having a rough time finding decent men.

The dating demographics and the cold winters seemed to be the only downside to living in Minneapolis. I loved my new apartment. It had one bedroom and beautiful French doors, arched windows and lovely built-in cabinets with glass fronts. I had absolutely no furniture, except a bed my dad had delivered. That's when, once more, I felt the hand of G!d.

Bill was a janitor at the apartment. He was a very slight man with a gaunt face and thinning, light brown hair. Bill had an interesting life story. He spent most of his life drunk, and then one day he woke up and decided that he would just stop drinking. And he did. He stayed sober for over twenty years after his vow to quit alcohol. No 12-Step program. He just quit. After he shared his story with me, we always exchanged nice words. I really liked him from the outset. He was aware that I didn't have any furniture and one day he came over to me quietly and asked me to follow him. We went to this huge basement area that had an incredible assortment of furniture. These were things people had put into storage years and years ago. Many of the items had been completely overlooked or forgotten.

Bill said. 'Help yourself to whatever you want, sweetie. Go ahead and furnish your apartment. These people will never be back for this stuff.'

What a sweetheart, and what a treasure! I stayed down there for hours and picked out a deep olive-green velvet couch and lovely mahogany tables. I carried the mahogany oblong coffee table up to my apartment and Bill helped me with the big stuff. I took lamps and night tables and three or four cool rugs, plus a really beautiful mahogany dresser with a matching mirror that looked perfect in my bedroom. I was so happy once my apartment was finally furnished. I don't know what I would've done without Bill's help.

The next big thing was for me to find a job. I had some experience working in natural food stores and decided this would probably be my best choice as I needed to stay away from the clubs and the accompanying temptations. I called a store and asked them if they had any openings, but they didn't. I refused to get discouraged and kept looking.

I decided to try downtown Minneapolis, and went walking down Nicollet Mall, just intending to familiarize myself with the area. There was a Gucci store that had the most beautiful shoes and purses in the window. Across the street I saw a health food store that included a restaurant called 'Naturally Yours', so I decided to check it out. I walked in and started browsing through the store's retail items. Almost immediately a tall, thin man called over to me, asking me if there was anything he could help me with. He looked like he was in the middle of trying to straighten out a display of vitamin bottles.

'Actually, I'm looking for a job.'

'Do you have any experience?'

'Yes sir, I used to work in health food stores in Maryland.'

'And do you have any management experience?'

I was thinking on my feet. I nodded. 'I can absolutely handle a management position if you have one available.'

Something had drawn me to this store, something was telling me I had to go there. As we talked, it became apparent to me that this was *bashert*, a Yiddish word meaning destiny. This was meant to be. I knew I was right where I was supposed to be, and that G!d was looking out for me.

I answered a few more questions and, of course, I was hired.

I thrived in the environment and the store did too. It was a delicatessen style store, a natural food carry-out with a small retail section stocked with supplements and books. I made natural fresh homemade soups every day. In addition, I baked natural breads, cookies and cakes in my apartment that I sold at the restaurant. We had an amazing Oster juicer that juiced one carrot per second, and an automatic orange squeezer. We sold fresh juices along with wonderful healthy foods. It was really an incredible operation and I loved it, I worked extremely hard to understand the retail products we carried and tried to help my customers as best I could.

One day a book order came in, featuring a large paperwork with a wild pink cover that was designed by Peter Max. I was really captivated by the cover and the title, *Survival into the 21st Century: Planetary Healers Manual*. I felt the same magnetic pull I had experienced with finding the store some weeks back. Once I opened it and started reading, I could not put the book down until I finished it.

The author was Viktoras Kulvinskas, and the book was a compendium of health practices, containing a lot of information about sprouting, juicing, healing foods and healing practices, and more. It had everything from acupuncture to Zen, and talked about philosophy, meditation and how to continue a lifestyle of health. As soon as I finished reading the book, I called the author and told him I was coming out to visit him.

'And where do you live?' he asked.

'Minneapolis.'

He laughed and told me that he lived over a thousand miles away in Woodstock Valley, Connecticut but that wasn't going to stop me. He told me I was welcome any time.

The next day I asked the owner of the health store for some time off. He reluctantly agreed, he could see how important this was for me. I also asked him for an advance on a week's wages because I had no money. The weeks wages covered the gas, with little left.

I was praying that Victor could help me recover from bulimia. It pained me that I had recovered from my drug abuse, but I was still spending hours binging and purging my food. I felt like a prisoner trapped in my food addiction. It was as if I had been transferred from one prison to another.

Victor greeted me with open arms. He was tall and extremely thin, with exceptionally long, light brown hair. He had deep-set eyes, which I attributed to his Lithuanian heritage. He was a little awkward looking, but exuded kindness. 'Welcome to the best day of the rest of your life.'

I knew this was going to be an adventure, and it was. I settled in for the night, sleeping on one of the bunkbeds.

Victor called his place Survival Foundation. It was a haven too beautiful to be believed. It was situated on a hundred acres of wooded land, had a large lake and a good size house, as well as a large barn that contained the publishing business. The place was a trip. There were beautiful murals on the walls, depicting Indian gods and goddesses. The kitchen had everything to create healthy fare. It was equipped with sprout bags; mesh bags one could grow seeds into edible sprouts. There were juicers and a Vitamix, a super blender that could pulverize anything. Plus, the smells were fantastic. There was always incense burning: patchouli, sandalwood, myrrh and other sweet aromas.

In the bathroom was a peppermint Dr. Bronner's soap. This was my introduction to the amazing world of Dr. Bronner. Not only did the soap feel fantastic, the bottle's label was covered with fine print proclaiming G!d as One, and more tiny prints that looked crazy but highly spiritual.

Everything at Survival Foundation was amazing. Viktor's book featured the basics of holistic living, with sections on sprouting and juicing and all kinds of information about natural healing practices, like massage and acupuncture. He had also discovered this elixir called wheatgrass juice, a chlorophyll-laden juice with incredible healing properties.

Victor was quite the guru who really loved anyone who came to him for healing. He was a truly remarkable man, with a wonderful energy. It felt like sitting in the sun when I was physically in his presence. He radiated a powerful energized warmth that was pure cosmic power and love. He followed the teachings of the Essene Gospel. The Essenes shared their possessions, lived by agriculture and handicrafts, rejected slavery and believed in the immortality of the soul. Their meals were always communal affair. Vik believed that any ailment could be cured with natural foods and natural healing. After I met him, I knew I wanted to follow his example and dedicate my life to helping and healing people in any way I could.

Of all the people I met on that trip, there was one particularly amazing woman who went by the name of White Dove. She always seemed to be cleaning and scurrying around helping others. She was only about five foot, three inches tall, very slender with a sweet but reserved face. I did get to spend a little time talking to her, though she was not very interested in talking. Later we would become dear friends.

I stayed with Vik for a week. There was no way I could absorb all his wisdom in such a short time, and I vowed to return. That was the beginning of a forty-year long friendship.

I was hoping that Victor was going to be the key to my release from bulimia. The first crack in the wall came when I noticed there was an enema bag in every bathroom. Enemas can be an element of bulimia if they are overused. The bulimic is fixated on removing food by vomiting, but can also use enemas and laxatives excessively to purge the body. It's really about getting rid of feelings. The food is just a metaphor. It's difficult to explain such a complicated psychological pathology. I knew it when I saw it, and I came to realize that Viktor was not going to be able to help me with my bulimia, per se. He did help me better understand nutrition and natural foods and healing practices, but the irony was that he was also bulimic. The difference was that he didn't think there was any problem with throwing up. At the time he thought it was a perfectly healthy way to resolve overeating. I was terribly disappointed, but completely amazed at what a wonderful person he was and how incredibly diverse this whole new universe was. He was a great listener and patiently spent hours with me that week. I knew this was a life-changing experience. I felt as if a palpable change had occurred inside me. Vik didn't have the magical fix for my bulimia but I believed he could help even though he had his own struggles. With a focused, healthier lifestyle and a new purpose I would beat it.

25

When I got back to Minneapolis, I threw myself into my work at the store and any spare time I had was spent helping people in AA any way I could.

I had volunteered to take responsibility for the whole foods for two upcoming AA events called Alcathons. An Alcathon is a huge party for recovering alcoholics and anyone else who wanted to party without drink and drugs. One event was scheduled for Thanksgiving and the other was set for New Year's. I was given a budget to purchase the food. Thanksgiving was for 1200 people and the New Year's event was for 10,000 people at the Minneapolis Football Stadium. To say it placed a lot of stress on me was an understatement. It was an incredible and overwhelming undertaking for somebody with new sobriety. I was very lucky to have the involvement of other members who put on the event and the experience taught me a lot about how to relate to other people.

We would begin our meetings by reading the twelve traditions of AA. These traditions served as a guideline for how the organization of AA functioned. This was different from the 12 Steps, which helps the individual recovering alcoholic to work on getting their life back. At first the meetings were relaxed and pleasant but as the events drew nearer and we concentrated more on the logistics of the event, I began to stress at the enormity of the task I had taken on, especially for the event at the Minneapolis Football Stadium. I started feeling overwhelmed and frightened I would not be up to the job

At one point I had a complete meltdown because I believed that I had blown all trust with everyone forever. I was given money to purchase the supplies. As you can imagine the budgets were fairly sizable. Around that time, I needed to get a new pair of boots and I thought it would be okay to borrow some money to pay for my boots. I had every intention of paying the money back as soon as I had my paycheck. Unfortunately, the paycheck was delayed. When I attended the next meeting, I burst into tears from the guilt. Fortunately, I was in a room full of loving people. They helped me understand that playing around with the money was old behavior and in coming clean I had a new start. I was so happy and uplifted. I knew that their fellowship was the best thing that ever happened to me. They lifted a huge weight from me with their love.

The Thanksgiving event was fabulous, it passed by with one small hitch. While I was slicing the celery, I managed to cut open my knuckle. I was moving too fast. The emergency room trip became dramatic when the initial doctor informed me he needed to call in a hand surgeon. I was terrified that I had damaged my ability to use my hand in the future.

When the hand surgeon stitched me up, I was told we wouldn't know how I'd do. We just had to wait and see. I was terrified, and over the weeks and months as my hand returned to normal function, the relief was immense.

Even with my hand bandaged and some of my movement restricted, I was able to pull off my part at the New Year's Alcathon. It was huge, with many celebrities attending and supporting the event and as the supervisor for whole foods I got to meet most of them backstage. I met Dick van Dyke and Art Linkletter, and was also introduced to a heavyweight boxer, Keith Ferguson. He was huge, six feet, ten inches tall, a walking tower of muscle. The chemistry between Keith and I was immediate and we began flirting with each other. He made a real play for me but I was hesitant. I could not stop thinking that as a giant who was nearly seven foot tall, his penis would be in proportion with his height. The thought of a giant penis really frightened me. Even though I was reticent, we nearly became an item. We dated a couple of times but thankfully never made it to the bedroom and I never did find out if a big body meant a big penis. What killed it for me was when Keith casually mentioned he had a boyfriend in Greenwich Village. The thought of him being bi-sexual really turned me off, and things ended.

I remembered my promise to G!d about serving women alcoholics, and one of my goals was to start an AA group within the women's federal prison in Shakopee, Minnesota. It was easy enough to set up, as I got the full backing of the prison counselor. When I called her, she told me she was in AA and welcomed the group. I drove a 125-mile round trip every week to honor my commitment. Ultimately, I started AA groups in the minimum security and the maximum-security areas and they were both very well attended. It is a well-known fact that a huge percentage of all prison inmates, both male and female, have struggled with drink and drugs, so there were no shortage of candidates for the groups.

Life was not easy for me. Even though I was sober I still struggled with bulimia. It would take many years of hard work for me to recover. After a couple of years living in Minneapolis, I moved back to the Washington area. There was nothing there for me, so when I spoke to Viktor and he invited me to New York to join him on his latest adventure, I was all in.

Vik wanted to start a yoga and healing raw food center in Kingston, NY. We were camped out at Oller's Mountain Lodge, and old no-tell motel that would have been perfect to house guests and staff for a healing center. There was Vik, me, David Steinberg, a real wheeler dealer that Vik had known for years, and a few other friends of Vik. Since we were located away from other properties and with enough privacy to suit us, the rule was that clothing was optional. It was spring and the weather was pleasant so if you chose not to dress then that was fine. The rooms were lined up in a row. Each unit had a bed, nightstand, dresser, and a small bathroom; simple but totally functional.

One of my most memorable moments came early one morning when I decided to walk over to Vik's room to talk to him about some personal issues that were troubling me. I always struggled with the rollercoaster of depression and as

Viktor was always patient when listening to my meltdowns, I decided to seek his counsel that morning. He always rose early to meditate and I knew he would be up, even though it was well before 6 o'clock. We all practiced yoga at random times of the day and one of the most popular series of poses is known as the Sun Salutation. As I opened my door, on my way to Vik's room, David and two other guys were outside and had just bent over, completely naked with their tushes facing me, as they were beginning the Sun Salutation. Three sets of swinging balls with accompanying anuses greeted me. Even if I live forever, I will never be able to erase that image from my mind. They thought nothing of my intrusion and proceeded as if I did not exist.

Sadly, the purchase of the lodge fell through. If it had been successful, I would have lived there and helped Vik in any way that I could. However, there I was, stuck in Kingston, with no plans and no money.

I had become quite good at massage and I thought I would try selling massages to sustain myself. I took out a small ad in the local paper, calling my work 'Esoteric Massage', and offering it for $25 an hour. Unfortunately, 'esoteric' is close enough to 'erotic', and I had to fight off my first few clients. I was repulsed by their sexual aggression. It seemed that rape still resonated in my subconscious. The thought of a man sexually aggressing me was totally repulsive. As it was, I generally needed to be pretty blitzed to take my clothes off and be vulnerable in a dating situation.

While I was carrying on selling my massages, I learned that a license was necessary to commercially practice massage in the state of New York. I investigated this and tried every way I could think of to get around the law. If you were ever busted for practicing massage without a license, you could never get a license to practice again. When all avenues of going around the law were exhausted, it dawned on me that I could go to school, get my degree and become a real therapist. Then I discovered that the cost of school was at least $7000, plus books and living expenses. I remembered that when my mom worked for the Maryland Department of Vocational Rehabilitation they had funding for people like me, who had physical or psychological handicaps, and needed training to become employable. I made an appointment with a New York Vocational Rehab counselor and got funded so I was in business. I attended The New Center for Holistic Education in Manhasset, Long Island. It was a 1000-hour course that took two years to complete.

For the first six months I lived with my aunt Audrey in Manhattan. The commute was a horror. My classes were at night, which meant I joined the mass business exodus as everyone returned to the suburbs in Long Island. I had to leave by 3:30 or I was cooked. If I waited until 3:31 my forty-minute commute turned into an hour and more. I could not believe people did this commute their entire lives. I sincerely could not handle the stress.

I want to pause my story for a minute to talk about my aunt Audrey. While it is true my relationships with my family has had ups and downs, there has not been a story as loving and ultimately as painful, as the one I endured with my aunt.

Growing up, I spent wonderful times visiting her home in New Rochelle, and spending time at her summer home in Fire Island. She was beautiful, tall ad curvy with long auburn hair. She always tried to give me a nudge to lose weight, which only added to my sense of self-hatred. When I was a teenager, she worked for the Village Voice newspaper, and got me free tickets to go to the shows at the Fillmore East where I saw Frank Zappa, Chicago and other major rock and roll bands. She even let me use her house while she was away for a weekend, a dream come true that I shared with a particularly hot boyfriend.

Unfortunately, if you fast forward to the end of my mother's life, my aunt found it necessary to commandeer my $150,000 inheritance, which my mother had promised me. Anyone who has ever struggled with family problems involving inheritances will understand what I suffered.

I had not realized how sick my mother became a year after she had a stroke. She was in her mid-eighties. My daughter Lisa had been born on Thanksgiving Day, and we had a tradition of flying out to my mother's for that holiday. It was always my mother's treat as I was a single parent and always struggled financially. I visited her once after her stroke, but other than the loss of her speech, she was fine. Just before her stroke, when we arrived for our annual visit, my mother greeted me by telling me she was leaving her money to Audrey.

'I didn't know you were dead yet,' was the only way I could respond. I didn't want to show her how hurt I felt. Later that night we talked. It seems Audrey was telling my mother how tough things were for her financially. I reminded my mother that Audrey lived in a million-dollar home in Santa Barbara, as opposed to our rented apartment, and that my inheritance was counted on to help secure my daughter's, her grandchild's, future. She said she understood and promised to leave things as they were with us inheriting the money.

Audrey spent a great deal of time with my mother during the final year of her life. It was a three-hour drive for her to visit Mom, as opposed to my flying coast to coast from South Carolina. I was not clear about how sick my mother was plus I really could not afford the expense and time off work if it were not urgent. As it turned out my stepfather was hiding the gravity of my mother's condition because he was becoming involved with her fifty-five-year-old caregiver. I had asked him to send me a picture of my mother so I could try to figure out how immediate the need was for me to go see her. That picture didn't arrive until after her death. When I received it, I was shocked to see my mother looking like a cadaver. Incidentally, my stepfather married the caregiver one week after my mother died.

All I know is that I was kept from having a final moment with my mother before she died. I was discouraged from coming out after her death because I was told she was cremated and the ceremony was short and not worth the trip.

Meanwhile, I had to deal with the pain of my aunt talking my mother into disinheriting me. When I tried to talk to her daughter, Sharon, about the unfairness of it all, she defended her mother, saying Audrey deserved the money because she spent time with my mother before she died. After she got the money, Audrey was insensitive enough to call me to tell me about a trip she planned to Europe. When she returned she called me to complain about what a miserable time she had. I remained civil to her, but decided it was better to stop talking. I tried to continue to communicate with Sharon, but since I would get so angry when she defended her mother I just had to cut ties with her as well.

Some time later I reached out to Sharon to try and mend fences because I knew my aunt was suffering from dementia and was hospitalized, but she basically seemed done with me. I'm sorry things degraded so much as to destroy family ties. I had been warned by others that inheritance disputes can get ugly, and I should have resolved this while my mother was alive. Let it be a lesson for all.

One last bit about another aspect of my inheritance. My mother had been quite a collector and had promised my daughter many beautiful items, including Lalique glass vases, stained glass and more. My brother Seton lived close to my mother and had easy access to all her collections. Though we had stopped talking for the last ten years or so, at the time of her death Seton said to me that my daughter and I would get nothing we claimed my mother promised us. Everything of value went to Seton and my stepfather and his new wife. My daughter and I received a rather pathetic collection of leftovers. You know all the junk you have left after you've removed all the good stuff in your home? That's what seemed to get boxed and shipped to me. Adding to the hurt was what I believed to be a piece of passive aggression in the way my stepfather boxed up the two cartons he shipped. The first box contained unbreakable stuff, including my grandfather's sword. That was packed in a solid box with a ton of bubble wrap. The second box, which contained some pottery and tangles of junk jewelry, was put in a flimsy box with a little bubble wrap. When the second box arrived, everything inside that could break, had. It felt like these shattered shards were a reminder of my mother's death and her broken body. It was quite upsetting.

Before my mother died people warned me that inheritance can be extremely explosive and toxic for families. While it is true I've heard many horror stories worse than mine, my best advice is to not assume that people will act thoughtfully and rationally. Greed can bring out real ugliness.

Back to my time in New York at massage school. After six months of classes, I moved in with my classmate's friend who lived near the school on Long Island. I massaged him in exchange for staying at his house which was only minutes away from the school, so it worked out well. I could escape the brutal commute from Audrey's place in Manhattan.

I wanted to return to Washington to start a massage practice, so in my final year of school I began the transition by spending half the week in New York and half in Washington. The commute was five hours in each direction and really took a toll on me. Often I would drive, binging and purging for the entire trip in both directions. While living in the Washington area, I did experience my first breakthrough with bulimia. I started the first Washington-area Overeaters Anonymous Group for anorexics and bulimics. I did this with the help of my dear Rabbi Lipman, who let me hold the first group meetings at Temple Sinai. Even though this did not herald the end of my struggle with bulimia, (that would come in my late forties), it significantly reduced the frequency of my binge/purge cycle. Even now as I read these words I am amazed that my addiction finally lost its death grip on my life.

Later I would start one of my most gratifying AA groups. It was at the detention center that was named after the judge who sentenced me to the Springfield State Psychiatric Hospital as a juvenile, Judge Alfred D Noyes. It was very hard to get any program started with juveniles, but because my probation officer, Rex Smith, went on to become the head of all juvenile services in Maryland, I was able to start the first AA group at the children's center, and probably the first AA group in any juvenile facility in Maryland or Washington D.C.

Around this time, I met and became romantically involved with Dr. David Wiggins, a psychiatrist in Bethesda. I was impressed with him as he had authored books, and was the quintessential Jewish prince, a Harvard graduate doctor. I lived with David for a while and helped him get involved with treating eating disorders. To that end, we started a group therapy practice, which I co-led with David. He was handsome, if not a little short at five feet, four inches. He was a Harvard University undergraduate, which impressed me to no end. However, he was lacking in organizational skills and I began taking over some of his responsibilities, mostly helping to ship out books to people who ordered them. During the period I worked with David I increased his earnings by nearly $100,000 through the eating disorder group I co-led. In addition to the group fees it also generated private patients for him.

Our relationship did not last and I left him.

Sadly, I later learned from one of his patients, a young woman named Gillian, that he had acted inappropriately with her, causing a great deal of damage in her life. While it is true that I only had her say so, what she confided in me and what I knew about David, made what she said wholly believable. Gillian said that after I left David still ran the group. After the group meetings, according to Gillian, David would have her stay and walk the dog and otherwise keep him company. Gillian was nineteen years old and attended the group because she had a weight issue. Her father was a doctor and paid to have her attend the group. Gillian said that she and David became quite close and that she fell completely in love with him. She said that he would occasionally put his arms around her in a strong embrace and say how much he cared for her.

I don't believe the intimacy progressed, as Gillian was not very attractive. I'm sure Gillian's keeping him company was simply a convenience. David had night terrors and could not stand being alone after dark. I'm sure he used Gillian to keep his demons at bay.

It wasn't long before David's attentions were directed towards his previous girlfriend, Pina, from his school days. Unknown to Gillian, a reconciliation was taking place. (He would later marry Pina.) Part of the condition of the reconciliation was that Gillian would need to go. David needed to get rid of her and told her so just before he went on a speaking trip to Berlin. He fired her from his group and barred her from coming to his house. Poor Gillian was horrified, David had made it perfectly clear that she was no longer needed and that he didn't care for her. However, while he was gone she thought she could endear herself to him by cleaning out the detached garage that had not been cleaned in over twenty years. She emptied the place of garbage, including two old broken toilets, polished his car and even polished the floor. Everything was immaculate. She thought he would be pleased.

When David returned he freaked out at the fact she was still around and looked for a quick fix to get rid of her. He looked around the garage and noticed that the toilets were gone. He asked her where they were and Gillian explained that she'd paid someone $50 to haul them away. David accused her of stealing them. At first Gillian thought he was joking. 'They were broken,' she said. 'They were beyond repair.'

David called the police and had her arrested for stealing the two toilets. Gillian explained that she paid someone to have them taken away to a garbage dump. Because she had taken them without David's permission, as incredible as it sounds, Gillian was jailed for a short period of time for theft on David's complaint.

Some time later she came to me and unwound this incredible tale of abuse. My heart went out to her. She confided that she had developed a self-destructive behavior in the aftermath of this crazy episode where she would whip herself with a belt. I was shocked but not surprised. I understood how she felt. On two or three occasions after we broke up, I felt remorse and tried to get back with him. He humiliated me terribly, and once or twice I hit myself to vent my anger.

When Gillian came to see me, I still had some of David's publicity photos which she wanted. I was glad to get rid of them.

I was torn in my opinions of David as a professional and a human being. I know that he strived to do good things in his life, and that was to his credit. However, reading his books on psychology was a huge disappoint. I felt that there was always a lack of authenticity about them. He would refer to himself as a great humanitarian, but how humane was his treatment of Gillian? It was a heartless ploy to rid himself of a malpractice embarrassment. Ultimately, I thought he was extremely selfish and self-centered, and I vowed to never forget Gillian. Every ten years or so I have tried to contact David, begging him to make some type of emotional restitution to Gillian, but he has successfully evaded me, taking no responsibility for the horrific damage he caused in her life. Strangely enough, some years later I had a massage client that was seduced by him when she was much younger. She was his pupil in a graduate class. I told her Gillian's story, and she was not surprised. He had seduced this woman as a student, and then unceremoniously dumped her those many years before.

I have no idea how Gillian is doing today. I pray she is well and hope she has found some sort of closure with though I doubt it. I've decided to start a Facebook page for women who have a story about David and want to share it.

The one wonderful thing that David did for me was to direct me to Dr. Herman Meyersburg. He had been recommended to David as a therapist for his own use. Dr. Meyersburg treated two types of patients, therapists and hard-core. Fortunately, when I met him, he recognized that I was unique and desperate. He took me on as a patient and worked with me to save my life. Without Dr. Meyersburg I never would have stood a chance of surviving. The first session I had I was still living with David, who paid for it. $125. When David and I broke up, I had no money. I was faced with the same situation when I was seeing the psychoanalyst while I lived at the Normans. When the Normans kicked me out I asked him if I could keep on seeing him. He told me Jewish Social Services had pulled the plug on financing me and therefore, since no one was going to pay his bill, he wouldn't see me. I begged him to help me, I needed him more than ever, but I had no money so he said he would not see me. I was crushed. What happened to all the care and concern he exuded when his costs had been covered? Once again I was facing the same dilemma. I explained I had no way to pay the $125 an hour to see him, so I assumed I was finished. As it turned out, Dr.

Meyersburg had started a clinic that served the community poor, called Mobile Medic. He said he had a slot for a psychiatric patient and he proceeded to care for me for close on twenty years for nothing. What a saint!

I liked to describe Dr. Meyersburg as older than G!d and twice as smart. It was through his loving care over the years that I was able to have the hope of true emotional health. Without his help I could never have hoped for a life filled with happiness. Though it took many years to achieve that happiness, it has finally come to me in my later years.

We are now up to 1986, and I have graduated from massage school and returned to live in the Washington D.C. area. While working I met John, the man who I would later become engaged to. I met him as a massage client, but on the first visit he said he was happy just to talk. He never got that massage. He was truly a smart, capable, but slightly crazy person. He looked like a short version of Walter Matthau. He had his own brand of appeal. Mostly I loved that he would thoughtfully cater to please me with bubble baths and shopping sprees. I wasn't in love, but I thought I was happy with someone who could bring me security. He took a job as a franchise salesperson for Damon's, a rib restaurant chain headquartered in Hilton Head Island, SC, and we moved there. Unfortunately, in less than a year it became apparent that he was more than just a heavy hitter when it came to booze. I did not want to be judgmental, so the fact that he drank Chivas Regal on the rocks every night was not enough to make me call him an alcoholic. Unfortunately, he got into a bad financial situation, became extremely stressed out and started drinking to the point of hallucinating. One night he accused me of stepping out of a limousine when I returned from an

AA meeting. In fact, my girlfriend had driven me from the meeting in her old battered car but John saw a limousine. He blew up in a fit of madness and returned to Washington and I stayed in Hilton Head, South Carolina. Prior to when he left, John had paid all the bills and we lived very well. When he left, I had only a couple of weeks left of paid rent in a furnished mansion we had been staying in. After that I was out on the street.

Through what I am sure was divine intervention, and some clever juggling, I survived to stay in Hilton Head, almost immediately developing a highly successful medical massage practice.

26

There was nothing of any real consequence that transpired in my first years in Hilton Head. I struggled with depression, and relapsed with bulimia at times. At a particularly low point I made an unsuccessful suicide attempt, but somehow I always kept striving to get better.

In 1991, the most important event of my life began to unfold. That was the birth of my daughter Lisa Ann. It certainly wasn't planned as I wasn't thinking about having a child. In fact, I had given up hope of motherhood once I hit forty a year before. Miraculously, I had somehow avoided pregnancy up to now, which was a minor miracle considering the number of times I had unprotected sex.

So, now at forty-one years of age, I'd missed a period and noticed my stomach was looking fat. 'Some sit-ups should fix that!'

I was wrong.

It never entered my mind I could be pregnant.

After a week or two I got suspicious, went to the local CVS and bought a pregnancy test kit. I couldn't wait until I got home so I used their bathroom. I tested positive for pregnancy. I bought another kit and used their bathroom again. Again, I tested positive. I couldn't believe it and returned to the store to buy another kit to take home. After the test I took home was positive, I made a doctor's appointment for the next day. It was inconceivable, I felt so inadequate. I couldn't possibly raise a child. I went to the doctor who confirmed my worst fear. I walked out of the building in a state of sheer disbelief. I'd lived such a catastrophic life. There was no way I could give my child a happy and emotionally healthy life.

Even though I felt like the worst candidate for motherhood, I determined I would do everything possible to be a good mother. I didn't smoke and I knocked off the bulimia. I wanted to do everything in my power to have a healthy baby.

Around the sixth month of my pregnancy I experienced a strange phenomenon. I was soaking in the bathtub when I saw a light slowly emanating from the faucet. It took on the appearance of smoke, but it seemed to be made of a cobalt-blue light. It slowly emerged from the faucet, and seemed to form a barrier. It was translucent, so I could see what was on the other side. The light seemed to form a force field that held back demons, small, gnarly, little beings that were trying to get to me and my baby. The experience seemed to last only a few minutes. Then, as quickly as it appeared, it disappeared. The blue light barrier withdrew into the faucet, as if it was sucked up, and it was all over.

Sadly, I became pregnant by a person with good genes but no future. I met my daughter's father in AA and was under the mistaken impression that he had been sober for a few years. It turned out he was clean when we were together for a few months, but almost immediately after I became pregnant he fell off and never put more than a year of clean time together in his entire life. Because he could not stay clean, I kept him away from my daughter with only a few exceptions. I did let him see Lisa twice when she was quite young, aged two and again at five. He was also invited to her high school graduation. My contact with him over the years was minimal and each time I saw him he just seemed sicker and sicker. His survival amazed me. Sadly, to the best of my knowledge he has never obtained sobriety.

Within six months of having my daughter I quit my massage practice. I would begin what I called my thirteen-year maternity leave. I could clearly see that there was no way I could be a good mother and run my practice at the same time. I knew it would be a struggle but I also realized that money was secondary when it came to the welfare of my child.

I moved back to Maryland as I could not afford Hilton Head without working. At the peak of my practice I was making up to $2,000 gross a week. I am convinced South Carolina hates poor people and there was no way welfare at $300+ a month could support us.

At first I relied on welfare. When Lisa was about three years old I got burnt out on being poor and tried to return to work for six months. Within that time, she developed Attention Deficit Disorder (ADD). She was diagnosed at the Hershey Medical Psychiatric Adolescent Unit in Hershey, Pennsylvania, so I knew it was real.

I had started seeing Dr. Meyersburg when I returned to Maryland and knew I had to get back to him with Lisa, to get help with her behavior. She would have terrible outbursts of anger that frightened me. He said that I had to quit working, so I did. He explained to me that she was deprived of my attention when I returned to work. Since I was the only parent, she needed twice as much of my attention, and I was giving her less.

It was Dr. Meyersburg who helped Lisa to fully recover, and without medication. He taught me how to parent her and really engaged with her in a meaningful way. He taught me that if I was on the phone, and she wanted to talk, Lisa came first and I should hang up. We would have a weekly session where we would play games like Chinese Checkers. It might sound a little silly but I'm convinced he taught me how to mother Lisa. When she would throw a tantrum, he would show me how to hold onto her until the anger passed. She quickly returned to her beautiful bubbly self. Lisa was the most charming, lovely child one can imagine.

Though she had no hair for the first two years (I called her my Buddha baby), she sported the most beautiful head of golden curls after that. She was outgoing and engaged everyone she met with her smiling face and charming ways. She was high energy and extremely precocious. She started walking and talking way ahead of the curve. She started walking at seven months and the most incredible phenomenon occurred when she was just two weeks old. Dr. Meyersburg claimed that babies could talk as young as a few days old and I tested that theory. I started training her to say hello from her first week. When she was about two weeks old, she said hell-o! A friend of mine, Michael Meyers, witnessed it one day, though he couldn't quite believe what he heard.

Raising my daughter as a single parent was never easy but it was always worth it.

27

I moved to York, Pennsylvania when Lisa was around eight years old. This was a city with a strong Jewish community and I needed that support. The temple was next door to the Jewish Community Center. I had everything I needed. The temple's rabbi was caring and greatly supportive. He even helped me out with money for the purchase of a car. The time Lisa and I spent at Sabbath services on Friday nights, and the times we joined in with the temple's congregation to celebrate holidays, meant a great deal to me. Being a part of a Jewish community helped me feel a part of something special. I spent my entire life feeling like an outsider and here I felt included and normal. A fellow among fellows.

One day I was standing at the reception desk at the JCC when a young nice-looking man asked staff for information. I detected a European accent, and intruded on the conversation. 'Excuse me, I cannot help but hear from the way you speak that you're not from around here. Do you mind if I ask where you are from?' I tried to sound casual, but as I found him to be cute, I was anxious to see if I could get connected with him.

'I'm from Denmark.'

I should have guessed. He was tall, well-built, and very blonde.

'Nice! I'd like to introduce myself, I'm Jan Kasmir.'

'Soren Morck'

'If I can do anything to help you find your way around, please let me know.' I had just moved to York, so the idea that I could do anything other than get him lost was silly.

'I am just joining the JCC to use the swimming pool.'

It only took us a moment to figure out we should visit his apartment when he was finished swimming. This was to be the introduction to my soon-to-be husband. In retrospect, I realize I shouldn't have married him. He was seventeen years younger than me. I think adopting him would have worked better, as it became apparent what he really wanted was a mother. Even though I was in my late forties, I was still extremely attractive and a real hot mama.

This relationship was doomed from the beginning. There were good aspects to the entire experience. We moved to Denmark, where my daughter readily learned the language. (I did not, as learning other languages was never a talent I possessed. Four years of studying French has enabled me to say about five sentences, with a strong accent.)

Unfortunately, my daughter absolutely hated Soren and they fought constantly. It was extremely difficult for him to secure adequate housing for us, as everything is enormously expensive in Denmark. It seemed doing almost anything in Denmark turned into an arduous task. According to Soren, even under the best of circumstances, renting a place to live takes a minimum of three months to arrange. I suspected he was making excuses for his own ineptitude, but as I knew nothing about Danish culture, I just tried to believe his excuses. He couldn't buy a car because they were too expensive. I really became inpatient with his excuses. It felt like I was asking a boy to do a man's job, and it really put a damper on our relationship. Sex was out of the question. I was totally turned off. For all my father's faults, growing up I always felt secure in the knowledge that my father was to be relied on for security issues like a house or a car. Of course, I didn't understand our marital problems, but looking back I can see I felt totally insecure trying to rely on Soren.

I have always had this idea that what I wanted most from a man was to feel small. I wanted to relax enough to stop being large and in charge. I wanted to let my man take control. I hope this is understood. I believe the ultimate gift of a good relationship was to relax and deflate. I am reminded of how an animal will inflate its size when threatened as a defense mechanism. Imagine going around inflated 24/7. That was me in most relationships. And with Soren, I was back to that unhappiness. I couldn't relax and feel small.

On the whole, living in Denmark for those two plus years was a wonderful experience. Sadly, it became apparent that Lisa and I could not tolerate staying in Denmark. My relationship with my husband was a bust. I could not speak

Danish, and even though most Danes spoke English, not speaking Danish was a huge barrier to navigating through any dealings with the Danish government. Having darkness all day in the peak of winter was depressing, and living in the south had conditioned me to hate cold weather. Denmark had real winter cold, and I hated that! It was time to go. I returned to Hilton Head in 2003.

It was a real struggle but I managed to work hard and re-establish my massage practice so that I could support Lisa adequately. Hilton Head is an extremely expensive place to live in and I had to work extremely hard, but I was fortunate enough to have a strong constitution and could keep up with our needs. My clients loved my informed ability to help them escape pain.

I attribute the effectiveness of my therapy to the incredible knowledge base I retained from my years of biology in college, the extensive training in extra massage techniques I received in workshops, plus the year I apprenticed with a physical therapist from Chicago, Carl Burdinie. The brilliant schooling I received in New York helped organize my knowledge to be able to treat pain issues with success.

There is one overriding factor I always find difficult to discuss, which I believe, is most important to my success in healing people. I have no doubt that I am a channel for G!d's love and healing energy.

When Lisa was in kindergarten, I tried to explain to her that Mommy was psychic. I have always had a psychic sensitivity that helped me connect to others without words. Part of doing my therapy is assessing my clients' issues by using my body to locate their pain. Instead of explaining all of this to Lisa, I tried to keep it simple. I just told her that 'Mommy was psychic'.

During a school conference that year, her kindergarten teacher explained to me that Lisa had shared with her that her mommy was 'psycho'. Ever since then the joke has been, 'Psycho or psychic?'

Looking back over my life, I believe it is fair to say that I have ultimately made my life a service. In big ways and small ways, when I have been healthy I have always tried to be of service to humanity. Some of the big commitments were the Ethiopian crisis in the 1980s, when I worked with the African Red Cross to try and get help for the starving peasants. There was my many years of service with the 12-Steps groups I started and nurtured, serving both juveniles and adults. I have used massage therapy as a service. During the 1986 Great Peace March in which people walked across the United States to support nuclear disarmament, I organized a group of people to greet the marchers upon their arrival in Washington D.C. When they arrived we massaged their feet. I've provided massages for the participants in the PTR wheelchair tennis tournament in Hilton Head since the eighties. I've never let money stand between me and taking care of a person, often offering people to pay just what they could for their massage, or giving it to them for free. More recently I helped five homeless women get housing by connecting them with local resources. That experience highlighted how disconnected helping organizations are and has helped me with ideas for my service after I retire from my business.

There's so many incredible events in my life that I want to share with people but for the sake of my first book I thought sharing my journey of survival was a great start. Now that you know I'm going to live and that I am a real person who spends each day as a working-class hero, I invite you all to let me hear from you. Please remember the important lessons that were hard won from the 60's. It's a sad and scary time we're living in. People are completely disconnected from the communities they live in. After learning to use Facebook I've never felt so liked and so alone at the same time, if that makes sense?

Mental health treatment is horribly neglected. Sadly, people suffering from mental illness don't know who to trust and have almost nowhere to go for help. I promise you there are answers and it starts with your community. Try to remember what it means to be a neighbor and then be a good neighbor! Don't forget that we are all in this together and without each other we are lost. My hope for strengthening the communities is Mensches in the Trenches. (A mensch is a person of integrity and honor.) This group is about supporting people who give of themselves to support, heal and promote the community.

In the future I hope to support the people who are making a difference in their communities through their actions, such as the people who start soup kitchens and the free health clinics, and inspire other people to follow their example. I believe it takes a village to raise a human being. If we can focus on the people who surround us and join to support each other we will get through anything. To this end, after the publication of my book, I will be focusing my efforts on developing my idea for community support. The fact is we have enough resources for everyone. If we could all come to the humble realization that we are our brothers' and sisters' keepers, things will start to change. Remember, be the change you want to see.

The greatest measure of my life is reflected in the health and well-being of my daughter, Lisa. I can proudly say that her twenty-eight year has seen her bearing the fruits of success in all aspects of her life. While she may not be perfect, whatever that looks like, she is so highly competent and successful that I could literally burst with pride. Her beauty shines through her physical, psychological and spiritual being.

She trained as a massage therapist and yoga instructor and has successfully taken over my business, guiding it beyond my wildest expectations of success. She has managed her physical health in a way that astounds me. Her commitment to a healthy, balanced diet keeps her looking stunning. She is not so rigid as to never eat a chocolate, which she enjoys immensely, but she is measured, happy and sane in her choices. Her weight is controlled and her muscles are toned, something I still struggle with at almost seventy.

She has made a wonderful choice with her boyfriend. Not only is he the sweetest, most thoughtful human I have met in a long time, he is handsome, funny and a commercial pilot, a highly desirable profession.

I cannot begin to express how deep my fears were about my competency as a parent. I feel completely assured that my eyes are open wide and I can believe my perceptions. I have worked long and hard on myself and my role as a parent. Mostly, I have applied my hippie credo, *Love is the answer.*

It is true that I will spend my final days carrying my message of Love and Peace. I believe it is also true that it will echo from the grave, living on in the single true message conveyed by my flower held out to the soldiers of the world.